Understanding the Tin Man

Also by William July II

Brothers, Lust and Love:
> *Thoughts on Manhood, Sex, and Romance*

UNDERSTANDING THE TIN MAN

Why So Many

Men Avoid

Intimacy

WILLIAM JULY II

BROADWAY BOOKS

NEW YORK

BROADWAY

A hardcover edition of this book was originally published in 1999 by Doubleday, a division of
Random House, Inc.

Broadway Books titles may be purchased for business or promotional use or for special sales.
For information, please write to: Special Markets Department, Random House, Inc., 1540
Broadway, New York, NY 10036.

BROADWAY BOOKS and its logo, a letter B bisected on the diagonal, are trademarks of
Broadway Books, a division of Random House, Inc.

Visit our website at www.broadwaybooks.com

First Broadway Books trade paperback edition published 2001.

Designed by Julie Duquet

The Library of Congress has cataloged the 1999 Doubleday edition as follows:
July, William.
Understanding the tin man: why so many men avoid intimacy/William July II.—1st ed.
p.   cm.
1. Men—Psychology.   2. Intimacy (Psychology)   I. Title.
BF692.5 .J85 1999
158'.081—dc21   99-046434

ISBN 0-7679-0566-0

01   02   03   04   05   10   9   8   7   6   5   4   3   2   1

To my mother and father.
Thanks for doing your best.

Contents

Acknowledgments   *xiii*

Introduction   *1*

Chapter 1   What's a Tin Man?   *5*

Chapter 2   How to Recognize Tin Speak   *21*

Chapter 3   How Men Translate What Women Say into Tin Speak   *31*

Chapter 4   Basic Types of Tin Men   *41*

Chapter 5   Men vs. Women   *51*

Chapter 6   Checking for Vital Signs: Emotional Numbness in Men   *61*

Chapter 7   Tin Man Jr.: How Boys Grow Up to Be Tin Men   *73*

Chapter 8   Sex: The Sweet Illusion   *85*

Chapter 9   Feminine Tin Speak   *95*

Chapter 10   The Tin Woman   *103*

Chapter 11   Macho-cide: Warning! Being a Tin Man Can Be Dangerous to Your Health!   *111*

Chapter 12   How the Tin Man Can Change   *123*

Chapter 13   A Woman's Touch   *133*

Chapter 14   "Honey, We Need to Talk"   *147*

Chapter 15 BUILDING THE BRIDGE TO INTIMACY,
ONE STEP AT A TIME   *157*

Chapter 16 TWENTY-EIGHT WAYS TO CHANGE YOUR
LIFE RIGHT NOW   *169*

Special Message 1 TO THE WOMEN WHO LOVE US:
A CONVERSATION ABOUT MEN
AND INTIMACY   *183*

Special Message 2 TO SINGLE MOTHERS   *185*

Special Message 3 TO AFRICAN AMERICAN MEN   *187*

Special Message 4 TO THE MEN OF THE
OLD SCHOOL   *189*

Special Message 5 TO THE YOUNG GUYS   *191*

THE MOST COMMONLY ASKED QUESTIONS ABOUT
TIN MEN   *193*

REALITY CHECKS: QUICK REFERENCE   *199*

BOOKS, MOVIES, AND PLAYS WITH TIN MAN— AND
TIN WOMAN—RELATED ISSUES   *201*

PLANNING A DISCUSSION   *205*

WHERE TO GO FOR HELP   *213*

WILLIAM JULY: ONLINE AND IN PERSON   *217*

PERMISSIONS   *219*

What good will it be for a man if he gains the whole world, yet forfeits

his soul? . . . what can a man give in exchange for his soul?

—Matthew 16:26

Acknowledgments

First, I humbly submit all honor to God. I am only an instrument for the Holy Spirit's power. The words in this book were from connection with the creator.

Love and thanks to my family: William July, Sr., Alice July, my sister, Jean Gist, and her husband, Lewis.

A special and loving thanks to my wife, Jamey, for her unyielding support of my life and work. She is not only my wife, she's still my girlfriend. I also thank her for suggesting the Tin Man metaphor a year ago when I was searching for an icon to symbolize my messages of male self-renewal. I also want to thank my stepdaughter, Laney, for all the humorous moments we've shared.

I extend my thanks to every person who bought *Brothers, Lust and Love*, making it a national bestseller. Especially those of you who told a friend to buy the book, too. And a special thanks to everyone who has come out to hear me speak. I look forward to more of those good times with you. A very special thanks to every person who has sent e-mail to my Web site. I appreciate your taking the time to directly share your affirmations, thoughts, and feelings about my work with me.

To the bookstores of America, thank you for all the orders, especially the bookstores who have been with me from the beginning.

I thank the many authors and speakers who've inspired me in my career—so many people that I dare not try to name them all! I particularly want to thank five authors whose words were part of the inspiration for this book: Royda Crose, Sam Keene, Dennis Kimbro, Jewel Diamond Taylor, and Iyanla Vanzant. Keep planting the seeds and spreading the positive energy! A special thanks to L. Frank Baum, author of *The Wizard of Oz* (from which I borrowed the Tin Man), for sharing his talent and insight with the world through a cast of quirky, yet profound, characters.

It would be difficult for me to write without jazz. As I wrote this book, the band played on well past quitting time. To the musicians who motivated and inspired me as I wrote this book, I send a big thanks. You are all truly instruments of God's energy: (in alphabetical order) Chick Corea, Miles Davis, Donald Fagen, Fourplay, Herbie Hancock, George Howard, Boney James, Earl Klugh, Eric Marienthal, Pat Methany, Marcus Miller, Rob Mullins, John Patitucci, and last but in no way least, Grover Washington, Jr.

I thank the Doubleday team for being so great to work with. A very special thanks to my editor, Janet Hill. She's a blessing to my career because she's that rare breed of person who possesses the ability to get down to business while retaining the creativity of a visionary. To my publicist, Patricia Blythe, many thanks for all your work on the front line. I also want to thank all of the people who move mountains behind the scenes: Roberta Spivak, the marketing team, legal department, sales reps, the copy editors involved in this project, the management, all the assistants, and the people in the mail room.

Last, I want to thank the pros who created the visuals. Thanks to Jean Traina for the cover design and Pam Francis for her sharp photography. I especially want to acknowledge my stylist, Nancy Chapman. Thanks to the looks she created for me on my last two book covers, you'd never know that I usually walk around in boots, jeans, and T-shirts.

Understanding the Tin Man

INTRODUCTION

Whenever the subject of relationships comes up, many women ask why so many men can connect physically or on the surface, but avoid deep levels of genuine intimacy. Frustrated, many women create their own answers to these questions. They say "men only want sex. They're designed that way." But is it that simple? Are men just emotionally numb robots who have no feelings and live for sex?

There are few things more dangerous than broadly brushed generalizations. First, all men aren't avoiding intimacy. Second, men are individuals and have to be approached as such. We're human beings with spirits first, then men. We are not only capable of achieving intimacy, we're equipped and designed for it.

But if that's the case, why do so many men avoid intimacy? The answer to that question may be found in society's age-old beliefs about manhood. Our society has long supported the view that being a man means that we have to conquer and control; make lots of money; have lots of women. Men must also learn to ignore physical or psychological pain; we pretend we don't have emotions. We men are groomed to only experience half of ourselves. But just because we've been trained that way doesn't mean that it's right or the best pattern by which to conduct our lives.

Many of us have felt the strain of the warrior mentality wearing us down and unraveling our lives. When I was on the road promoting *Brothers, Lust and Love*, I recall a conversation I had with a radio producer in between segments. He asked me what my next book, *Understanding the Tin Man* was about. I said, "It's about how some men avoid intimacy because we've been taught that our manhood is defined by our ability to dominate and have power over our surroundings. Intimacy is the opposite of that: It involves interdependence and sharing. Since most men have been trained to maintain control at all times, we tend to avoid intimacy. But by denying our own emotions and feelings many of us travel down a self-destructive path that leads to promiscuity, addiction, neglect of our health, and overall unhappiness. After we wear ourselves out, we realize there's something missing and decide we need to establish a new and healthy approach to life." I thought the rugged-looking producer would be turned off by the idea of men needing to be more sensitive and connected to their lives, but I was wrong. He nodded his head in agreement. Then he stroked his beard and uttered a deep "Mmm hmm. . . . You're right. I know exactly what you mean."

I've had that same reaction from men of all ages, incomes, and ethnic backgrounds every time I bring up the topics in *Understanding the Tin Man*; we all feel that our lives and relationships must change, but we haven't given ourselves the permission to break out of the mold. Society hasn't allowed us the freedom either, and so we remain the same and we live by a definition of manhood that leaves us stressed out. We then seek solace in sex, money, drinking, getting high, or develop an insatiable desire for power and control. But those things only lead to more of nothing. Some men can never have enough alcohol, drugs, sex, money, or power to make them feel complete. We have to turn the equation inside out; develop what's inside. By putting our lives in balance and developing the right perspective, we can enjoy our lives with increased health and prosperity.

We need a new paradigm for manhood. A new model of manhood for a new millennium. A manhood shaped by wholeness, balancing masculine with sensitivity and connection. A replacement for the obsolete idea of manhood that has left us out of balance, disconnected, incomplete, and in many cases, utterly self-destructive. While this is a major shift I'm talking about, I do want to emphasize an important fact: *This book is not a formula for the feminization of manhood.* I love being a man. I love being masculine. And I don't think women want men to be more feminine either. Just more human!

I'm a recovering Tin Man myself. The pages of this book aren't filled with sociological or psychological theories. I'm speaking as a man who has traveled this road. I'm living proof that disconnecting from the typical macho thinking and combining wholeness and sensitivity with masculinity will change everything in a man's life for the better.

Seven years ago, being an author was only a dream for me. I was pursuing two full-time careers: a police officer by day and a realtor in my off-time. As if working at two full-time careers wasn't enough, I had a third career as a freelance magazine writer. I was the poster boy for stress. My mind was always tied in knots because I was running it in fifth gear all day and night. Though I loved working out, I rarely found the time to exercise. Eating well was impossible. My breakfast, lunch, and dinner were fast food. Nutrition for me was a multivitamin with my pizza, followed by cake for dessert. My personal life was a mess, too. I avoided having a real girlfriend, preferring to limit my social life to shallow sexual encounters.

On the surface I looked successful and happy as I cruised around in my Mustang convertible. I had money in my pocket and a career that represented power and commanded respect. But I could feel myself unraveling inside. I was tired, unfulfilled, and burning out fast. In quiet moments with myself, I planned to somehow make an escape from my own life. I didn't know what I'd do or how I'd do it, but I knew things couldn't remain the same. Everything came to a head one morning while I was on duty. The dispatcher came on my radio and told me to call in for an emergency message. My father had had a heart attack. I sped to the hospital and rushed to his room. Standing by his bedside with tears in my eyes, I lectured him about learning to relax. I told him that he was trying to do too many things at once. I told him that he was killing himself. Then I realized I was doing the same thing. If I didn't change my ways, thirty years later I would have a son standing over me delivering the same message. Would he be doomed to the same path, too?

That was just one of a sequence of pivotal shifts in my life. That experience and others combined to transform my thoughts and beliefs about manhood into a more balanced and healthy perspective. By the grace of God I was on the road to recovery from self-destructive living. The seeds of change had been planted in my mind. The realization that I could and should change frightened me at first, then it filled me with confidence and determination. Those thoughts transformed me from a Tin Man into a whole, emotionally accessible man. I disconnected from casual sexual relationships and started dating and eventually consecrated a spiritually based marriage. I no longer just dream of being an author—I'm an award-winning, bestselling author. I don't neglect my body anymore; I honor it with exercise, massages, and better nutrition. I no longer worship the false god of money and "success"; instead I'm doing what I love for a living and everything is taking its divine order.

My previous life seems like decades ago, but it wasn't even ten years ago. And it would still be my reality today if certain events hadn't woken me up to the need for a new direction in my life. I pray that men and women both will read this book with open hearts and minds. For some this book will be an affirmation of what they're already doing. But for others it will provide the seeds of change. Seeds that will grow into thoughts that will become engines of transformation. Personal transformations not only change us as individuals, they also change those around us and, as a result, the entire world. However, such changes in individuals and the world don't happen instantly or without challenges. Growing has never been synonymous with instant gratification. Still, it is synonymous with peace, wellness, and contentment. After all, isn't it better to change and grow than to remain the same and self-destruct?

Chapter 1

What's a Tin Man?

I Don't Need a Doctor!

A Chicago bus driver had been complaining of chest pains for several months. One Monday morning, he told his wife about particularly uncomfortable chest pains and tightness in his left arm. Still ignoring the symptoms, he went to work anyway. Suddenly, while driving his regular bus route, he collapsed from a heart attack. When the paramedics arrived the bus driver was dead.

Drawing a Line in the Sand

Two men in a pristine subdivision of Houston were embattled in a bitter property line feud. For months, their anger had intensified. One of the men even went so far as to install a security camera to make sure his neighbor didn't cross his property line. But his camera's most valuable images turned out to be from a violent encounter with his neighbor. As usual the hostile words flew; but this time his neighbor decided to finish the fight by beating him with a shovel. The entire matter made its way to court and on to the national news.

You've Got to Be Kidding

The comedian Sinbad once told a joke about a Los Angeles man who was ashamed to tell his girlfriend that he'd lost his job. The man feared that having lost his job would lower his status as a man in her eyes. Instead of facing the facts and telling her what happened, he decided to cover up his unemployment by robbing a bank!

Sometimes I think we men are crazy. Why does it take extreme situations for us to see that we're killing ourselves with macho attitudes? Notice, I said "we men," because I'm including myself. Similar to the men in the above examples, my revelations about manhood didn't just drop out of the sky. After years of macho thinking I finally saw the light. A couple of years ago I had a harrowing experience that involved my health; a situation in which I almost died as a result of my own macho thinking. It took a life-threatening experience to force me to understand what being a man really meant.

Like most men, I believed that being a macho "tough everything out" type of guy was the essence of manhood, but I was wrong. Being macho is the best way to self-destruct. In fact, that's one reason women live on average seven years longer than men, according to Royda Crose, Ph.D., author of *Why Women Live Longer Than Men*. Crose also pinpoints some of the factors that influence male self-destructive behavior in the name of "manhood." She says, ". . . some men cling tenaciously to macho images of invulnerability, power, violence, and dominance. The demands of sustaining these images lead some men to self-destructive behaviors—Type A hostility and aggression, alcohol and drug abuse, cigarette smoking, and denial of pain or illness."

After I almost lost my life due to my own hard macho head, I knew it was time to reassess my opinions of exactly what made me a man. Since there aren't many male self-help or self-renewal books available, I did lots of thinking. I thought about my childhood, I reexamined my teen years, and I thought about many of the different decisions I'd made in my adult life. I talked with men and women I knew and got their opinions; I also canvassed experts. Combining all of that information with my own experiences, I discovered that there was a Tin Man living inside of me and inside many men of all ages and backgrounds.

The Tin Man Is More Than a Fictional Character from *The Wizard of Oz*

You're probably wondering what a Tin Man is. At first mention, the comparison of macho male behavior to the Tin Man may not be obvious. Most people associate the character from *The Wizard of Oz* with Munchkins, witches, and funny costumes. But underneath the whimsical dancing and singing, there's a more profound meaning to one of the world's most popular stories.

In the book, *Sisterfriends*, author and motivational speaker Jewel Diamond Taylor explains the hidden symbolism and imagery at work behind the scenes in *The Wizard of Oz*. She says, "In the past I had given my power away so many times looking for something outside of myself to make me happy, to tell me what, when and how to do something or simply failed to listen to my own inner voice. As I began to heal my broken pieces, dissolve illusions, become spiritually aware and develop self-esteem, the subliminal message of Dorothy's journey to Oz became clear and relevant in my life."

For men, it's the Tin Man's journey to Oz that holds a special meaning. The Tin Man joins Dorothy, the Lion, and the Scarecrow on the trip to Oz to see the Wizard because he wants a heart. Like all the other characters in the movie, the Tin Man believes the Wizard has some magical power to give him what he's missing. This, of course, begs the question: Why doesn't the Tin Man have a heart? According to the legend of the Tin Man in the book, the Tin Man was a woodsman whose ax became cursed, causing him to turn the ax on himself. As he hacked away at himself, he became covered in tin; eventually he hacked away his own heart.

My interpretation of that for men of today is that the ax represents our belief that being manly is to live by conquest and to seek power and control. The self-destructive hacking represents what this obsession with power and control does to us spiritually, mentally, and physically. The lack of a heart represents our separation from our completeness. We strive to master the physical, external side of ourselves; while neglecting the inner man—the part of us that needs intimate and strong human relationships to thrive. The tear frozen on the Tin Man's cheek represents our petrified feelings. All men have feelings and emotions inside. Some may have buried them, but they do have them; after all, we are human.

But our connection with our emotions gets trampled early in life when it gets in the way of the macho manhood myth, the delusion that we aren't men if we don't conquer, control, and rule over everything around us (i.e., build a harem, have a job that gives us power over other people and important things). Like the woodsman who became the Tin Man, we've cut away our feelings and become petrified in our own self-destructive beliefs about manhood. And that's precisely my definition of a Tin Man.

A Tin Man is any man who believes his total worth as a man is based on his ability to conquer and control other people through means of sex, money, physical power, or manipulation.

I can imagine that many men are stepping back and saying, "not me." But our methods aren't always obvious, even to ourselves. Men who walk around with their chests stuck out and a scowl on their faces are obvious Tin Men. But Tin Man traits aren't just about the way things look. They're actually about what's going on inside. Sometimes, the true Tin Man identity of some men is strategically well hidden because our society has traditionally celebrated the results of male conquest and control as characteristics of heroes.

For example, a man who sacrifices all of his personal relationships in order to rise in his career is a Tin Man. Yet he may be celebrated as a brilliant businessman. A man who can connect with many women physically, but in no other way, is a Tin Man. But he's patted on the back and called a "lady's man." A man who is overly possessive and domineering with his wife and kids is a Tin Man. But he may say that he's just doing his job as the man of the house. A man who avoids taking care of his health is a Tin Man, although he may be seen by many as a real man who can tough it out. Tin Men come in many forms and have a wide variety of motives, some of which may even be honorable in their intent. But all of the reasons boil down to attempting to be invincible and in absolute control, things that are impossible for all people, even the Tin Man.

Takes One to Know One

As I've said, I'm not writing all this as a casual observer. I'm not preaching and shaking my finger at Tin Men either. Instead, I'm talking as one of them. I'm a Tin Man myself. Actually, I consider myself a recovering Tin Man because I've identified my own self-destructive macho habits, arrested them, and begun the healing process. I'm blessed that I turned myself around early in life. I credit my dogged determination to rise to the top as quickly as possible, i.e., to be a man as defined by our society—powerful and in control. The fast-track lifestyle taught me some lessons about what's really important in life. When I think of my previous compulsively ambitious life in the fast lane, a life that was speeding me toward a spiritual, mental, and physical crash, three specific situations come to mind.

One was my career. I was working too much. I had bought

into the false god of a good job and secure career. The belief that even if I worked myself until I developed high blood pressure, I'd be able to relax and enjoy my material rewards at some point in the future. I measured my worth by the money I could make and the growing length of my résumé.

Second, my relationships with women were entirely off center. I simply didn't have much of a relationship with women outside the bedroom. I had grown accustomed to having sex with women while remaining emotionally detached. It was almost like a sport to me. I just wanted sex to satisfy my physical desires and bolster my ego. I'd become emotionally numb.

Finally, I was literally killing myself spiritually, mentally, and physically. I enjoyed eating sweets and hearty meals. I was consuming too much fat, too much sodium, and too many high-calorie, nutritionally unsound foods. On top of that, I was ignoring the warning signs of high blood pressure. Spiritually and mentally, I was neglecting to take time to retreat from the rat race. I avoided relaxation, meditation, prayer, and other practices critical to good health. Ultimately I put my life in danger because I, like most men, didn't go to the doctor when my body was telling me it was in a state of emergency. (In the chapter "Macho-cide: Warning! Being a Tin Man Can Be Dangerous to Your Health!" I discuss the issue all men are eventually faced with, and the harrowing experience that changed my life.

Don't get me wrong: I didn't change overnight. Personal transformation is a process that takes months or years—for some men, a lifetime. It's an intimate sequence of steps that we undertake at our own pace. There's a Buddhist saying, "When the student is ready, the teacher will appear." That certainly applied to me. When I was ready, the changes in my life came rapidly. I stopped having meaningless physical relationships with women when I realized that emotionally detached sex was doing me more harm than good, and it wasn't helping anyone else either.

Through experiences of hurting and being hurt, I learned that a relationship was an emotional and spiritual connection of which sex was only a small part, not the meaning of the relationship itself. I stopped overworking when I realized that I had a limit to the amount of stress I could handle. I learned it wasn't always possible to "tough it out" all the time. And from illness, I learned that I wasn't invincible.

Being a Whole Man

Today, and throughout the history of humankind, men and women have been raised with a different set of values. The separation begins at birth. Boys are dressed in blue. Girls are dressed in pink. Boys are encouraged to roam and explore—go outside to play ball, wrestle, and get sweaty. Meanwhile girls are encouraged to be delicate, neat, and soft-spoken. Boys are told only sissies cry. Girls are told it's okay to cry. Unfortunately, our current social climate teaches boys to believe that their ability to conquer will determine their place in the world. Equally unfortunate is that our current social climate encourages girls, both directly and indirectly, to determine their worth by their ability to attract men or be caretakers. Hence, the old adage, "Men grow up wanting to conquer the world. Women grow up wanting to conquer men."

Certainly, men and women are physically and psychologically different. Thank God! Everything in the universe was created with an equal opposite: light and dark, cold and hot, birth and death. Yet in all those opposites, there is oneness. The Tao symbol of yin and yang reflects this with the interlocked symbolic link of masculine and feminine. It's a universal law as old as time that isn't about to change. I'm not disputing that. Rather, I'm encouraging men to flow with it.

> Reality Check #1: *Men and women aren't intended to be exactly the same. We're complementary opposites.*

We're dangerously incomplete without development of our full selves. It's sort of like when you go to the gym and you see a guy who has a cast-iron chest, bowling ball–size triceps and biceps, but skinny, undeveloped legs. Overall, he's not as strong as he could be, he's not balanced. He's overtrained his chest and arms and neglected his legs. The result is an odd-looking physique that can't function to its maximum efficiency. It's the same with our emotional lives. We can't function as full men by ignoring our rage, frustration, vulnerabilities, or sorrows. Whether we men want to admit it or not, we have a sensitive and emotional part of ourselves that we need to cultivate in order to have more complete and healthy lives. When we get to the point that we would rather have a drink to drown our feelings in liquor, punch out our raging feelings on another person, or place ourselves into a woman's body for reasons other than love, we're in trouble. That's exactly where we are today.

It's time for a change.

Can This Feelings Stuff Go Too Far?

Don't expect to walk into the gym and see a muscle-bound bodybuilder crying on the bench press because he can't lift the barbell.

I don't think we're ever going to see construction workers riveting a skyscraper together and boo-hooing because the foreman just cussed them out for being behind schedule.

Imagine the Denver Broncos' Terrell Davis fumbling the ball, taking off his helmet, and bursting into tears. It's not going to happen!

Don't expect overworked oil field roughnecks to demand a

break from their work so they can set a white linen table for high tea. Forget about it!

I'm not suggesting that men become whining, sobbing, namby-pambies who are obsessed with being in touch with their feminine side! But there are a whole host of emotions that men need to acknowledge, understand, and learn how to process in healthy ways.

Women Have Bought into the Macho Myth, Too

"Boys will be boys" is what many women often say. Women are not free of responsibility for some of these male issues. In fact, they're willing participants in much of the macho male belief system. Some women are often culprits in the very schemes they say they want to end. I often hear two messages from many women. I hear them saying they want sensitive, caring, and faithful men in their lives. But then I see them doing things that contradict what they've said. I see them putting up with anything and everything from a man just to keep him. I see them putting down sensitive "nice guys" in favor of playboys and macho-man types. And I see many women happily accepting the role of "the other woman" when they know a man is married or committed.

Of course, I'm not talking about all women. But there are many who willingly allow men (and themselves) to remain in the dark when it comes to accountability to ourselves and others in relationships and life. Such women are "Tin Women." Below are the types of Tin Women that are discussed later in the chapter "The Tin Woman":

- *The Fixer*
  The woman who gives her all to others and has nothing left for herself.
- *The Happy "Other Woman"*
  The woman who prefers to date married/committed

men and lives in denial about what she's doing to
herself.

- *The Gold Digger*
This is the woman who only dates men who will open
their wallets for her.

- *Ms. Ego*
The woman whose answer to everything is "I'm a strong
professional woman who doesn't need anybody for
anything."

- *Daddy Drama*
This woman's looking for a daddy in all the wrong
places.

- *Ms. Ice*
She's cold and ruthless, and breaking hearts is a game.

- *The Scorned Woman*
She's angry about her past and holds all men responsible
for one man's actions.

- *The Man-Chasing Mommy*
More concerned about getting a husband than taking
care of her kids.

- *The Henpecker*
She's determined to "make" a man act the way she wants
him to.

Tin Women are similar to Tin Men in that they believe they
must conquer or control people in their lives. Some do this pas-
sively, while others have a more active strategy. Perhaps it's in
response to the harshness of the male-dominated world that
they've chosen to acquire many of the traits of the Tin Man as a
means of survival. However, this doesn't mean they aren't feminine. And it doesn't have to do with profession, income, or sexual orientation. It doesn't have to do with whether or not they are
feminists either. It's all in the attitude. Tin Women are those

women who have assumed a macho stance toward life similar to that of Tin Men.

One example of a Tin Woman in action was the ruthless character Meredith Johnson, played by Demi Moore in the film *Disclosure*. After being scorned in a secret workplace love affair by Tom Sanders, played by Michael Douglas, Meredith turns into a manipulative and ruthless executive with little regard for the feelings and lives of others in her climb to the top. She is a woman who takes on the macho, conquer-at-all-cost attitude of many men, and in so doing she becomes a Tin Woman. To some, that might not sound like a bad idea for a woman who wants to protect herself in a male-dominated world. But imitating men who are destroying themselves isn't a good idea. *Women who follow a female version of the macho manhood myth are marching off a cliff right behind the Tin Men.*

Tin Women can also have a passive method of bravado. An example of this type of Tin Woman would be the tireless self-sacrificing matriarch who has to raise her kids after a husband walks out on her. Against the odds, she works hard and sacrifices to raise her children and they grow up to be successful. She becomes self-sufficient because everyone is depending on her. But often in that situation, the mother becomes so accustomed to tending to the needs of others, that she, like the Tin Man, learns to avoid her own feelings in an attempt (albeit well intentioned) to carry the load for everyone else.

This book looks at the Tin Man and the Tin Woman because self-renewal for one can't take place without the other side following. Some men need a new approach to life and some women need a new approach to men. When men change, women have to change. When women change, men have to change. It's as natural as day and night. See the chapter, "A Woman's Touch."

Creating a Balanced Male Lifestyle

Can men live a balanced lifestyle? Can men be "manly" and experience the power of their emotions too? The answer is yes. It is critical to the spiritual, mental, and physical health of men to make adjustments in the areas of our lives that are slowly and silently killing us.

Striking a spiritual, mental, and physical balance is the key to life. But it's important to realize that we are out of balance in the first place. We have to identify the Tin Man in us. We have to admit that we are separated from our emotions and desperately need to reconnect with ourselves. I now invite every man reading this book to take the Tin Man Quiz. Ladies, I invite you to give the quiz to a man you know or love. But beware: If you question your husband or boyfriend directly, the answers you receive may not be totally candid. But don't worry, because you have raised the issues.

The Tin Man Quiz

Answer the following questions as true or false:

1. The best way to make up after an argument is sex.
2. My favorite way to celebrate is by having sex.
3. Sex is my preferred method of easing my mind and relaxing.
4. Coming from a girlfriend/wife, the words "we need to talk" make me uncomfortable.
5. For an evening to be intimate, it must involve sex.
6. A man should always earn more than his wife/ girlfriend.
7. Married women shouldn't want or need to work.
8. It's my job to do the driving when I'm with a woman.
9. Birth control is only the woman's concern.

10. Women need a man's help when making big decisions.

11. Even if the man and woman both work full-time, it's the woman's job to wash clothes, cook, do the dishes, and take care of the kids.

12. The sight of gay men angers me.

13. Housework is the woman's responsibility.

14. A man fulfills his obligations in a marriage by working, paying the bills, tending the yard, repairing things around the house, and having sex with his wife.

15. Men can have other women on the side if they take care of home first.

16. I've had a nagging medical symptom for weeks/months/years but I haven't been to the doctor because I don't think it's anything significant.

17. I only go to the doctor when I'm very ill, injured, or if it's required by my job.

18. I maintain sexual relationships with several women so I'm always able to get sex when I need it.

19. The next best thing to sex is a good stiff drink/drugs/a big meal with a rich dessert.

20. I'll never back down from a fight.

21. Having a female supervisor is an insult.

22. Asking for help (i.e., asking for directions when lost) is a sign of weakness.

23. Sex isn't as much fun if I don't have someone to brag to about it later.

24. The women I meet could never measure up to the standards of women like my mother or grandmother.

25. I'm very critical of men who try to date my female relatives and friends.

26. I have more experimental and expressive sex with women I'm not emotionally attached to.

27. If a woman makes me really angry, I'll grab, push, shake, or hit her.

Score Card

(A "True" response to #27 automatically equals a DIE-Hard Tin Man—definition follows)

0–1 True responses = Not a Tin Man

2–4 True responses = Recovering Tin Man

5–9 True responses = Open-Minded Tin Man

The open-minded Tin Man is generally regarded as sensitive and a good conversationalist who isn't too hung up on machismo. (But beware: The Tin Man beliefs are lurking just beneath the surface.)

10–15 True responses = Hard-Core Tin Man

The Hard-Core Tin Man believes in the macho, traditional type of manhood. He can be domineering at times because he feels men should always be in control of things. This man doesn't generally approve of blatant womanizing, but he believes "boys will be boys."

16 or more True responses = DIE-Hard Tin Man

The *DIE*-hard (*D*estroying *I*nner *E*motions) Tin Man believes men are superior beings. He is domineering, hardheaded, possessive, and could be potentially abusive. He rarely shows any emotions other than anger. He sees womanizing as an inherent right and privilege of manhood.

Things to Think About

1. Ladies, was any new information or insight revealed to you? Are you involved with a Tin Man?

2. Men, do you see yourself in the definition of the Tin Man? What did the quiz make you think about?

3. Can men go too far in expressing their emotions? If yes, what would be an example of going too far?

TRY THIS
For Women
When a man cries or expresses fear, pain, or vulnerability, are you uncomfortable? What is going too far for men when expressing their emotions?

TRY THIS
For Men
Think about the last time you were really feeling down about something, something that really hurt you inside. How did you handle it? Talk it out with a friend? Have a drink? Have sex? Did you hold it inside? Did your way of handling the issue bring you peace or temporary gratification?

Chapter 2

HOW TO RECOGNIZE TIN SPEAK

At my workshops, I often listen to women complain about men who don't want to commit or who turned out to be very different from how they first appeared. This is certainly the truth in many cases. But there are also many cases in which the problem isn't simply a lying and cheating man. *Some women want a man so badly that they overlook the red flags and warning signs that tell them to avoid certain men.* Then, when the truth of the situation finally explodes, the women seem shocked and stunned that the men they wanted so badly turned out to be monsters, cheaters, or financially unstable. But often the evidence was there from the very beginning.

> Reality Check #2: *There comes a time when there are no victims, only volunteers.*

"Fool me once, shame on you. Fool me twice, shame on me." We can chalk up one or two romantic disasters to experience. But if a woman continuously falls into bad relationships (especially with the same types of men), she needs to reexamine herself first.

Iyanla Vanzant offers straightforward truth on the subject of understanding why we choose to be involved with the people we have relationships with. Vanzant says honest self-examination leads us to the truth about our relationships. In her book *In the Meantime*, she says, "You will recognize yourself in what is going on around you. You will realize that you have attracted the emotionally unavailable person, the abusive person, the unsupportive person. You will recognize that you seem the most interested in the very person who is not the least bit interested in you. You will understand all the things you have done to try to make an unworkable situation workable. You will eventually become aware that your experiences are the result of what you have been thinking, saying, and doing."

I also like the way Marianne Williamson breaks it down to the core in her book *A Return to Love*. Williamson says, "Women say to me sometimes, 'Marianne, why do I always meet emotionally abusive men?' My answer is usually the following: 'The problem is not that you met him—the problem is that you gave him your number.' " She goes on to say, "The problem, in other words, is not that we attract a certain kind of person, but rather, that we are attracted to a certain kind of person."

Reality Check #3: *It's not always about what someone else does wrong to us, as much as it's about what we are going to do right for ourselves.*

How many women out there are reading the obvious signs men give away about themselves? How many women are really listening to the words men use? How many are just hearing what they want to hear from the lips of men? Contrary to popular belief, men often say *exactly* what they're thinking. But that's only if you're prepared to decode it. *The first step in decoding what men say (Tin Speak) doesn't even involve men; the first step is to be honest and courageous about who you are and what you want. The second step is to actually evaluate what men are saying without adding your own thoughts, feelings, and desires to it.*

This chapter focuses in on the many obvious verbal clues that men give about their intentions. As I said earlier, lots of women overlook these obvious danger signs when their romantic feelings start to cloud their judgment. As a result, many women fall victim to the belief they can change a man, train a man, or get him "right."

But that isn't the case. Men who aren't ready for relationships shouldn't be coaxed into them. How do you know who these men are? They'll tell you. Their words will literally tell you what they mean. What women must learn to do with men is *stop*, look, and *listen*: Open your eyes to see, tune your ears to listen, and sharpen your ability to work from the voice you hear deep inside you telling you what's right and wrong.

Just listen to what the Tin Man is telling you. Once he opens his mouth, you've got a direct line. It's often said that a woman will tell a complete stranger her life story. Well, it's no less true for men; women just haven't been listening. The Tin Man's language is coded but precise. His words are never meaningless. Behind his words are hidden feelings, emotions, and energy. Never take them lightly.

Tin Speak

Tin Men communicate via a coded language called Tin Speak— the complex and ambiguous art of male double-talk. It's so deceptive that Tin Speakers even start believing the words they're hiding behind!

Tin Speak allows men to avoid dealing with their feelings and relationships. Another reason a man resorts to Tin Speak is in an attempt to get what he wants without having to commit himself in any way. And the least culpable reason is that some men just don't know what to do with the feelings churning inside them; therefore, they don't know how to put them into words.

How to Crack the Code

As a recovering Tin Man, I know the language well and I've translated the code into standard English in this section. Below, you'll find a list of the most common Tin Speak phrases. I've also added a Warning Scale to indicate just how dangerous and volatile a relationship with each of the Tin Men could be.

Below are several typical Tin Speak comments. Each is followed by a Warning Scale rating—the number indicates how much drama he can cause in your life on a scale of 1 to 10 (10 being a catastrophe), an interpretation of what the statement means, and some brief reflections on the statement.

1. I'M NOT READY FOR A RELATIONSHIP.　WARNING SCALE 9
Translation: *I'm not ready for a relationship, but I'll have sex with you.*
Okay, at least he's honest. This guy is telling you up front that he's actively avoiding a relationship. It appears that he's using plain English, but actually it's Tin Speak. Tin Men say, "I'm not ready for a relationship," but continue to pursue a woman as if they do want a relationship. Such men either just want to have sex, or they're looking for a date who's available on demand. But remember, if he's told you he doesn't want a commitment, he doesn't want a commitment. So don't waste your time creating delusions of a relationship. Don't try to rationalize what he said. Don't think you can change him.

2. I HAVEN'T MET THE　　　　　　WARNING SCALE 7
RIGHT WOMAN YET.
Translation: *I don't know what I'm looking for in a woman.*
Does this guy have a realistic view of women, or is he waiting for some fictitious Ms. Perfect to pop out of the sky? Probably no woman can measure up to his unrealistic view. Even if he gets into a relationship this man most likely will always believe there's a better woman out there that he's missing out on.

3. WOMEN TODAY ARE A PAIN.   WARNING SCALE 7

Translation: *I'm difficult to get along with.*

If his perception is that all women are too difficult for him to be in a relationship with, maybe *he's* the one who is too difficult to get along with. It takes two to tango. This kind of man often tells stories of how crazy his ex-girlfriends are and why he had to leave them. But if he always seems to be involved with "crazy" women, what does that say about him?

4. I DON'T WANT TO GET SERIOUS.   WARNING SCALE 9

Translation: *I don't want to deal with all the responsibilities of a relationship.*

This guy may be a great date and lots of fun, but he's hesitant about taking it to the next level, a committed relationship. Hats off to this man for being honest. He probably really means that he doesn't know if he can handle a monogamous relationship and all of the responsibilities that come with that—sharing his feelings, opening his heart, etc. Or, he may not feel a serious relationship is best for him right now. Guess what? You can't change him! Let him grow into himself and check back with him later if you're still interested. Don't push him. If you do, you're setting yourself up for a big fall and you'll have nobody to blame but yourself.

5. I'M CONFUSED RIGHT NOW.   WARNING SCALE 9

Translation: *I'm confused and I'll probably hurt you.*

Yes he's confused, but at least he's honest. The good thing is that confusion is often a state of transition. Perhaps he's starting to sort out complicated issues in his life. Who knows? But the fact remains, he's in a period of change and you should wait until he's ready before you try to get involved with him. That could be months or years; but whatever you do, don't try to rescue him!

Reality Check #4: *A good relationship has everything to do with timing.*

6. I NEED SPACE.   WARNING SCALE 8
Translation: *Several possibilities. (See list below.)*

1. *You're not the one for me, but I like having you around.*
2. *I don't want to get into anything serious, but let's keep having sex because I'm enjoying it.*
3. *Thank you. You've been a delicious "flavor of the month." Now I'm outta here.*
4. *I'm going to go out and see other women, but I want to hold on to you in case I want to come back.*
5. *I love you, but I need to sort some things out.*

Use caution with this last one. Some men are simply trying to drop out of sight. And some legitimately need time to think some things over. Everyone needs space in a relationship, even married couples. Don't deprive him of the right to be alone or he'll just resent you. But if you think it's an excuse to play the field, that's another matter altogether. Follow your instincts.

7. YOU JUST DON'T UNDERSTAND ME.   WARNING SCALE 9
Translation: *I can't communicate what I'm feeling.*
You probably *don't* understand what he's feeling inside. Can we ever fully understand another person? He might not understand himself either. It could be the tip of an emotional iceberg. Until he can sort out his own feelings and express what's wrong with him, he's not a safe emotional harbor for your feelings.

8. I WANT TO REACH MY CAREER WARNING SCALE 8
GOALS BEFORE GETTING INTO
A RELATIONSHIP.

Translation: *My* top priority *is to achieve my career goals and dreams.*
This guy is trying to get established in life, and for some men that's
a very important issue. This man wants to have a solid start in his
career and a strong sense of direction in life before he makes commitments to another person. Even if you don't agree with him,
you should heed his words. He's telling you what his priorities are.
He's also telling you where you stand in those priorities; at best,
you're in second place. A serious relationship with this guy would
only lead to frustration.

9. I'VE BEEN HURT BEFORE. WARNING SCALE 9
Translation: *I don't trust women.*
We men don't handle emotional pain well. Yielding to our feelings requires us to become vulnerable. Nobody likes to be vulnerable, especially Tin Men. When we finally get the courage to
give our feelings a chance, we're taking a big risk. If we get hurt
in the process (even a little bit), we draw back inside, terrified of
being hurt again. A hurting man will hide his feelings, lash out in
anger, or even be unfaithful as a way to deal with his pain.

10. I'M JUST A DOG, I ADMIT IT. WARNING SCALE 10
Translation: *I'm looking for a casual sex partner. May I borrow your
body tonight?*
No ifs, ands, or buts about it, this guy's definitely not looking for
a friendly conversation, a date, or a relationship. He wants to
come over at midnight and leave by three A.M. for a "slam, bam,
thank you ma'am." Sure, there's a human being suffocating
somewhere inside that canine costume, but that's not the point.
Listen to what he's saying. This man is a hot stove that will burn
you!

11. I'M MARRIED, BUT . . .   WARNING SCALE 10+

Translation: *I'm looking for some extramarital fun and games. Are you willing to be my play toy?*

If he's married but flirting with the intent to start an affair, he told you he was married for one of three reasons:

    a. He thinks it's cute that he's married and playing around,

    b. It's a hint for you to keep things discreet, or

    c. He feels guilty.

No matter what the reason, seeing a married man is a waste of time. It's simple: This man is unavailable; he's committed emotionally, physically, and financially. But still I've heard women rationalize the situation and say such things as, "he doesn't love his wife anymore," or "he's only in his marriage for the sake of his children," or "it's just a little fling for fun." Whatever the excuse, it doesn't pan out. Seeing a married man ultimately reaps no benefits.

A Final Note: When it comes to avoiding our feelings, men are pros. Our actions and words generally don't leave much to the imagination. Again, don't assume anything. Don't try to interpret what *you* think he means. Don't rationalize for him. Don't add a "but" or an "if" where he didn't put one. Just *stop*, look, and listen . . . *think,* then act.

It's so important that this point bears repeating. No matter how cute he is, how fine he is, how good the sex is, how great the conversation, how much money he makes, or how dreamy you feel snuggled in his arms, learn to read the man's situation for what it really is. Everything that feels good isn't good for you.

Things to Think About

Women

1. Do I believe being in love means that I have to throw caution to the wind?

2. When in love, do I hear what I want to hear, or do I listen to the facts?

3. Has a man ever told me something up front that I ignored only to be blasted by it later?

4. Have I ever ignored obvious questionable characteristics or actions of a man only to have them come back and haunt me?

Men

1. Do I play word games with women to hide my true feelings or motives?

2. Do I tell women what I think they want to hear to get what I want?

3. Do I have trouble communicating my feelings to women?

TRY THIS

For Women

In a previous or current relationship, have you ever ignored your intuition about any of the following?

1. You see signs early on that he is a playboy, a freeloader, or an abusive person.

2. He becomes disinterested in you after his promotion, graduation, or new job.

3. He is more interested in having sex than he is in going out on dates.

4. You get a feeling he might be married or otherwise committed, and then find out he is.

TRY THIS
For Men
Read the following statements and think about what you've said in these situations. What did you say when:
1. You wanted to make an exit from a relationship that wasn't working?

2. You wanted to cover up your infidelity?

3. You were hurt inside by something she said or did?

4. You enjoyed the sex but didn't want a relationship?

5. You didn't want to get serious?

6. You wanted to get serious?

7. You wanted to know how she felt about you?

In those situations, did you communicate what you were really thinking?

Chapter 3

How Men Translate What Women Say into Tin Speak

Not only does the Tin Man speak a foreign language, the meaning of simple things is often lost on him; he can't comprehend words and phrases as they're spoken to him without first translating them into his native tongue, Tin Speak. Unfortunately for women, the Tin Man misunderstands lots of conversations because they get blocked or bent into another form by his ego.

Following are some examples of common phrases spoken by women that lose their meaning when men translate standard English into Tin Speak.

What Tin Men Think They Hear from Women

SHE SAYS   TIN MAN HEARS
1. We need to talk.   *You're in trouble.*

James dropped his girlfriend, Diane, off at her house. After escorting her inside, he got back in the car and headed home. A few minutes later, his car phone rang, he turned down the music, and answered. "James, it's Diane. We need to talk." James felt a lump in his throat, his heart raced at one hundred miles per hour. Thoughts rapidly flooded his mind: *I just left her house five minutes ago. What could I have done wrong so fast? Why is she mad at me?*

The Tin Man has difficulty communicating without frustration or confrontation. For more on communication, see the chapter " 'Honey, We Need to Talk.' "

SHE SAYS   TIN MAN HEARS
2. Would you like to come over tonight?   *Let's have sex.*

Carl and Erica had been going out for two months. It was obvious that they both liked each other a lot and he'd long been fantasizing about having a sexual relationship with her. But he knew Erica was serious about keeping sex out of the picture until she knew him better and they had time to build a relationship based on love and not just lust.

That's why he was shocked when Erica invited him over to her apartment for dinner on the evening of his birthday. Upon hearing the invitation, Carl hung up the phone and jumped in the shower. He slipped into his "special occasion" black silk underwear and doused himself *everywhere* with cologne. On the way over, he stopped and bought a package of his favorite condoms and tucked them inside his leather jacket. He was ready for a romantic evening.

The Tin Man's idea of romance is sex.

SHE SAYS   TIN MAN HEARS
3. I want you to meet some of my friends.   *I want to show off that*
                                              we're a couple.

Patrick and Amber had only been dating a couple of weeks when Amber received an invitation to a dinner party given by close friends. Although she was still getting to know Patrick, she thought he would make an ideal date for a dinner party because of his outgoing personality. He was witty and could tell jokes almost as well as a stand-up comedian. And the fact that he was tall, dark, and handsome also made him the perfect date.

Amber had a couple of other options, but Patrick was at the

top of her list. She pictured a fun and light evening full of laughter, friends, and good food. From her point of view it would be a great opportunity to have a friendly date without lots of pressure. Besides, she thought, regardless of their possible relationship, he'd just be fun to hang out with. Amber picked up the phone and called him.

"Hi, Pat, it's Amber. What are you doing on Saturday?"

"Nothing, but I'd love to see you again. Let's have dinner."

"That's just what I had in mind. I've been invited to a dinner party on Saturday and I wanted to know if you'd like to be my date. I want you to meet some of my friends."

A pause. "Oh, well, I meant dinner as in the two of us. I'm not sure about going to a dinner party with your friends, Amber. I mean, I don't know if I'm ready to start meeting your friends, family, and all that stuff. Let's just take it slow at first."

"Pat, I asked you to a dinner party. I didn't ask you to marry me!"

The Tin Man believes all women are out to trap him into a relationship.

SHE SAYS	TIN MAN HEARS
4. Hello.	*I'm attracted to you.*

Marcus stepped into the office in a new custom-tailored suit, sporting a clean haircut and freshly trimmed mustache. He was happy because today he was interviewing for a position as a department head. The office rumor was that he was a shoo-in for the big promotion because of his outstanding sales record. Soon Marcus would be out of his cubicle and in his own office.

He felt like a winner and was exuding a warm radiance as he walked into the copy room to run off a few things and get a head start on the day. Standing in the room was Andrea, a coworker he had often seen around the office but had never really introduced himself to. She was an attractive woman with closely cropped hair delicately framing her dimpled cheeks. She was dressed in a skirt that conservatively complemented her long, well-toned legs.

Marcus's and Andrea's eyes met, and Andrea flashed a big friendly smile and said, "Hello." Marcus took this as a sign of more than just a "friendly" hello. He immediately opened the conversation with a comment about her shapely legs and stepped flirtatiously close to her, *a very dangerous move for the workplace.*

The Tin Man doesn't understand that a woman can be friendly without being flirtatious.

SHE SAYS	TIN MAN HEARS
5. *I want to talk about our sex life.*	*You're not a good lover. A real man can satisfy a woman every time.*

Tonya and Rick lay in bed staring at the ceiling. Rick yawned with satisfaction and patted Tonya on the thigh. Tonya's lips were pursed and she had tears welling in her eyes. *He did it again. Rick can be so selfish,* she thought. *He never considers what I need from our sex life.* She was trying to figure out how to approach the subject without his getting angry again. The last time she asked him if they could work on his holding off ejaculation longer, he stormed out of the bedroom and wouldn't talk to her for two days. She didn't want that to happen, so a tear slid down her cheek and onto the pillow as she turned away from him to face the wall.

But she was raging inside. It wasn't fair for her to feel so unsatisfied in the bedroom all the time. Over five years, she'd had three kids with Rick and couldn't even remember having as many orgasms with him. She sat up and wiped the tears from her eyes. "Rick, I want to talk about our sex life."

The Tin Man wants to believe that he's Superman under the sheets.

SHE SAYS	TIN MAN HEARS
6. *You scare me when you get angry.*	*I like strong men.*

Robert was a man of average height and build, but he had a giant temper. Frustrations from work, creditors calling, and lingering child visitation problems with his ex-wife had taken their toll on his nerves over the past three years. Robert had started drinking more than his usual amount and he was becoming more belligerent toward everyone, especially Kim, his wife. She was actually beginning to fear Robert because he was becoming increasingly hostile—frequently resorting to foul language, threatening creditors on the phone, and flying into a violent rage whenever his ex-wife's attorney would contact him.

One afternoon, after a shouting match with a collection agency over a furniture bill, Robert flew into a rage. Kim asked him to calm down and said, "Robert, you scare me when you get this angry." But Robert marched right by her and smashed his fist through the living room wall.

The Tin Man believes physical power is a large part of being a man.

SHE SAYS	TIN MAN HEARS
7. *I wish you would surprise me with candy or flowers when it's not a special occasion.*	*You don't do enough for me.* *You don't appreciate me.*

Although he always bought roses on Valentine's Day, bought great Christmas presents, and remembered the birthday of his girlfriend, Lisa, John never considered himself a romantic. But in their year and a half together, Lisa felt a formality about John's gift giving, almost as though it were his duty. One evening as they sat in the park, they watched another couple leave the flower stand and stroll along the lake. The girl had an armful of carnations. Lisa said, "That's so romantic."

"I bought you flowers with your birthday gift, baby," John said defensively.

Lisa turned to face John. "But he probably got her those for no reason."

John waved his hands in disbelief. "Naw, it's probably her birthday or something."

The Tin Man thinks he has romance all figured out but actually
doesn't have a clue.

SHE SAYS	TIN MAN HEARS
8. *Maybe we should ask for directions.*	*You're not man enough to handle this situation.*

Carol and Jeff were running late for her sister's Saturday afternoon birthday party. Since it was a surprise party, they needed to
arrive on time. Jeff was winding around the long, quiet streets of
the Baltimore suburb searching for the right place to turn. He followed every street on the map, but still couldn't find Cherry
Blossom Road, the street on which Carol's sister and her husband
had just built their new home. As they followed the map and cir-
cled the neighborhood for the second time, Carol noticed a
woman working in her yard.

"Jeff, let's ask her how to find Cherry Blossom Road."

"I'll find it. I have a map. It should be around the next corner."

"That's what you said twenty minutes ago. We're going to
miss the surprise!" Carol snapped.

But Jeff kept driving as though Carol hadn't said anything. After another ten minutes, Carol had a suggestion. The development
was divided into two sections by a bridge. Since they'd had no luck
finding it on one section, she figured it must be on the other side.
"Jeff, let's try the neighborhood on the other side of the bridge."

"Carol, I know what I'm doing. It couldn't be on the other
side. There's nothing on the map on that side."

Finally, after almost an hour, and passing the woman working
in her yard four times, a frustrated Jeff agreed to pull over to let
Carol ask the woman for directions.

"Excuse me, ma'am. Could you tell us how to find Cherry
Blossom Road?"

The woman put down her rake and approached the car. "Oh,
that's easy. It's the only street on the other side of the bridge. It's

new so you won't find it on that map you have. Just go across the bridge and turn right," she said, pointing in the opposite direction they were heading.

By the time Carol and Jeff arrived at the party, the surprise was over, the cake was cut, and the champagne was gone.

The Tin Man sees asking for help as weakness.

SHE SAYS	TIN MAN HEARS
9. *Can you help me with a big decision?*	*I'm not strong enough to handle this situation by myself— I need you to take control.*

When I was in real estate, I had lots of deals killed by Tin Men. One such case was that of a young single CPA whom I showed a home in suburban Houston. This woman, whom I'll call Andrea, absolutely loved the home for its bright kitchen, remodeled bathrooms, and cozy bedrooms. The house was perfectly appointed, and ready for move-in. When I told her the owner had been transferred out of state and had reduced the price for a quick sale, she was especially excited. Andrea was poised to sign and make an offer for the home, but she wanted her boyfriend to see the place first.

Early the next morning, I met Andrea and her boyfriend, Rod, at the house. He was a tall, well-dressed man who shook my hand extra hard and said hello in a quick and formal clip. From the curb he stared at the house and asked me how old the roof was. The roof was practically new, but before I could say anything, he said, "Write a new roof in the contract, or no deal." Andrea looked at me and then at Rod, and waited for his next comment. I knew *exactly* where this was going.

Next, Rod wanted a new paint job and landscaping. Once inside, he wanted the walls in the living room resurfaced. He thought all the ceiling fans needed to be replaced. And he even said the recently remodeled bathrooms looked old. He didn't know what he was talking about, but that didn't matter. Within twenty minutes, this man had talked Andrea out of a great investment.

This scenario was not new to me. I'd been in the real estate business for years and the deal-dashing "know-it-all" Tin Man was just another occupational hazard. I knew his type well. The reason Andrea's boyfriend didn't like the house had nothing to do with the house—anyone could see it was a good deal. Rod killed the sale because he wanted to control Andrea. He didn't like the fact that Andrea had considered making a big decision without his prior input.

The Tin Man must always be in control.

Things to Think About

1. Did you recognize yourself in any of the scenarios in this chapter?

2. What issues or discussions cause you to "shut down" and not listen to your significant other?

3. Do you shift the focus of the conversation if you're criticized? Do you try to bring up counterarguments or unrelated things?

4. Do you replay conversations in your head and sometimes find that you were wrong? Do you apologize?

5. How can you be a better listener?

TRY THIS
For Women
1. Identify some situations in your life in which you didn't listen to what your husband or boyfriend was trying to tell you because your ego got in the way.

2. Think of some ways in which the women in this chapter could have communicated their feelings and thoughts more effectively, while still being diplomatic.

TRY THIS
For Men
1. Identify some situations in your life in which you didn't listen to what your wife or girlfriend was trying to tell you because your ego got in the way.

2. Think of some ways in which the men in this chapter could have communicated their feelings and thoughts more effectively, while still being diplomatic.

Chapter 4

BASIC TYPES OF TIN MEN

It would be difficult, if not impossible, to label and describe every specific type of Tin Man. However, most Tin Men fall into general categories. This chapter identifies some of those basic categories by profiling the thoughts of a Tin Man type typical to each category. Let's explore the minds of these Tin Men.

The Commitment Avoider

I'm not saying that I'm not ever going to get into a serious relationship. In fact I want to do that . . . one day. But right now I just want to have some fun. I like coming and going as I please and not having to answer to anybody. Besides, when you don't get serious, you also don't have to worry about hurting somebody's feelings. That's why I keep it light. If a woman gets all serious on me, I back off until she realizes, if that doesn't work, it's later for her.

I'm dating three different women. One is for when I feel casual. She's my pal, my movies-and-popcorn girl. She's also the one I can talk to if I just need a friend. The second is my uptown girl, she's sexy and classy. I call her up when I want to get dressed and go out to look good. My third girl is my wild thing. She likes to get crazy in bed. Like me, she just wants to have a good time. We don't even date. We just call each other up when we feel the need.

I have just the life I want. I have my freedom, three great

women, and no strings attached. Why would I ruin that by starting a relationship with just one woman?

Note: Married men or men in long-term relationships can fit into
this category as well.

The "Nice" Guy

Some guys will lie to a woman to get what they want, but I never
do that. I believe in respecting women. That's why I'm always
honest and up front with them about everything. If they ask me if
I'm dating other people, I say yes. If they don't ask, I bring it up.

I'm not a dog. But I do like the ladies. I definitely have my fun
with women. I make no apologies for that and I shouldn't. Every
woman I've ever been with has known where I was coming from
in the beginning. When we sleep together or date, they already
know it's not a relationship. And all of them have accepted that
with the exceptions of the women who made the mistake of
thinking they could change me. I don't think I'm doing anything
that any other eligible bachelor isn't doing. There would be
something wrong with a young single man who didn't enjoy the
pleasures of several women.

But like I said, I'm not a dog. I know that a woman likes to
talk, snuggle, and be appreciated. I send cards and flowers to my
ladies. I let them know I appreciate them. I'm not like all the
other guys. I'm a nice guy.

The Player

I have only one goal: sex. I don't want to talk. I don't want
to listen. I don't want to date. I just want sex. To get sex I will
lie, cheat, or say and do just about anything I have to. It's not
always easy to spot me because I have so many disguises. I can

be nice, charming, seductive, or pretend to just be a "friend." But all I want to do is have sex. Don't expect me to lie around and pretend to be tender afterward either. And I'm definitely not going to spend the night. Don't waste my time if you're not game. Any questions?

Note: Some players are married or already in relationships.

The Robot

I'll be totally honest with you. I've been married for ten years to a woman I love and I have two children that mean the world to me. But I woke up the other day, looked in the mirror, and I didn't know the man I saw. I feel as though I'm stuck playing the leading role in somebody else's life.

I have a steady job that takes care of my family well and I'm due for a pay raise at the end of this year. But I never wanted this job. I took it twelve years ago with the intention of doing it until I could get something better going. But then came children, then a house, and all the other expenses that come with being a family. It takes every cent that my wife and I make working full-time to pay our bills. Every day it's the same routine. I feel trapped. I wish I could do something with my life that would provide for my family and make me happy, too. I have dreams of starting my own business, but I don't know how I can make that move with all the responsibilities I have. I'm a good man and I'd never in a million years walk out on my family. I'd never even let them know that I feel this way. But I'm tired and frustrated. Something has to change to keep me from giving up hope and turning into a zombie.

The Hard Worker

My work is my life. It means more to me than anything. It's the one thing in my life that makes me feel excited and satisfied. I know that sounds bad, but my wife and I stopped having a real relationship many years ago. We're just two strangers who sleep in the same bed. Since I'm at work all the time my kids are strangers to me for the most part, too. But to tell you the truth, that doesn't bother me because I know I'm a good man. Last year, I put my wife in a new Range Rover. I bought her a diamond tennis bracelet and paid for her and the kids to spend a week in the Virgin Islands. My kids only wear designer clothes and I'm saving to send them to Ivy League schools.

Honestly, I don't really have much free time. One of the most pleasurable parts of my day is driving my Mercedes convertible home after work. Although it's kind of sad that by the time I'm finished with one of my ten- or twelve-hour days, I'm too tired and wound up to even put my top down for the drive home. But hey, that's the price of success.

The "Good" Man

I came home late from work last night and saw the most beautiful thing I've ever seen. Michelle and my one-year-old son were asleep together on the bed. I looked at the motor oil all over my hands and under my fingernails, and realized it was worth it. Every hot, sweaty moment at the garage repairing cars was worth it. Every backbreaking crate I moved on my night job at the warehouse was worth it. I'm the man of the house. My wife is my queen and my son is a prince. I pay all the bills, solve all the problems, fix anything that breaks, play with my son every day, and still make love to my wife enough to keep her satisfied.

I'm not going to lie. It's tough. To be honest about it, sometimes I think it's killing me. "Tired" wouldn't begin to describe my aching muscles and throbbing headaches. Michelle knows I'm working myself too hard. Last year she asked me if I thought she should get a job to help out with the bills and I flatly told her no. I'm the man of the house. It's my job to provide and that's what I'm going to do. I told her that no wife of mine would ever work. I'd rather work myself to death than have my wife take a job to help support us.

The Gigolo

I know how to get a woman. You shower her with affection, bathe her in attention, and make love to her until she begs you to stop. Then you can get anything you want. A woman in love doesn't care about money, her car, or her home. What's hers is yours, especially if nobody has ever really made her feel loved and special. If you need some money, she'll give until she's broke. If you need transportation, she'll loan you her car. If you need a place to stay, just say the word and she'll move you into her place.

I know, because I've done it over and over with more women than I can remember. Sometimes it's for small things, but this corporate executive I'm living with is my biggest catch ever. When I met her she was lonely, divorced, and horny. I took care of her needs and she fell in love with me. I've been living with this woman for two years now and I haven't worked a full-time job since I met her. She travels all the time and you know I've turned this house into a playpen when she's gone. I've had women right here in the house all night. This is the life. She's even going to pay my tuition for barber school.

The Power Freak

I'm in control. I'm the boss and everybody bows to me. It feels great to walk into the office in the morning knowing that there's nobody greater than I. People rush to open doors for me. They all want to speak to me. A nod of my head or wink of my eye means everything to people because they know that I can create or end careers.

The source of my power is fear. Everything I do creates an environment of intimidation and insecurity among my subordinates. This keeps everyone off balance. They always wonder what I'm thinking, how I'm feeling, or if I'm watching over their shoulder. Creating this kind of fear in a person allows me to get whatever I want.

Note: A man doesn't necessarily have to be famous, powerful, or wealthy to be a power freak. Some men display this behavior in their personal or family relationships.

The Tough Guy

I'm a real man because I don't take any shit from anybody. That also means that I never back down from fights, because I'm no coward. The way I see it, a man has to stand his ground or people will run over him and then he'll never get any respect. People respect me because they know that I can and will kick some ass.

The Obsessor/Possessor

If you don't keep a woman under control, she'll do anything. I keep an eye on everything my woman does. If she's at work, I call to check up on her. When she's at her mother's house, I call to see if she's really there. She complains and calls me possessive and insecure, but I don't care. I keep doing it. As long as she isn't cheating, she doesn't have to worry, right?

If I ever catch her cheating, she'll be sorry. But I don't worry about that, because I keep a close eye on her. I'm even watching her when we go places. I watch her to see who she's looking at. I listen to how she speaks to other men. If I don't like what I see or hear, I ask her about it. When I do, you better believe I'm checking for lies.

The Addict

It started simply enough. At first I just used it as a way to ease my mind. When I was stressed, it delivered relief. When I was afraid, it gave me courage. When I was angry, it made me happy. If I felt small, it made me big. But then I began to depend on it. Now I'm at the point that I need it just to feel normal. I can't seem to get enough. The more I get, the more I want and need. It has taken over my mind. I live for it. Now I feel desperate and I know I'm out of control, but what can I do?

Note: This person could be addicted to sex, drugs, alcohol, or even food.

In addition to the profiles in this chapter, here's a simple and practical guide to some other characteristics that identify the basic types of Tin Men.

Ten Characteristics of a Tin Man

1. Would rather be lost and late than ask someone for help or directions.
2. Hogs the shared armrest in movies or on airplanes (particularly when seated next to other men).

3. Sizes people up. Stands erect with chest stuck out to intimidate or impress other people.

4. Stares at people in an attempt to intimidate them or prove he's not afraid.

5. Scowls. Walks around with a frown on his face believing it makes him look tough.

6. Will never sit with his back to the door.

7. Will not turn sideways when passing people in tight spaces.

8. Talks in a hard and loud tone to create an air of power and confidence.

9. Flirts aggressively. Flirts to the point that it's uncomfortable, offensive, and/or borders on illegal.

10. Becomes inexplicably infuriated by the sight of gay men.

Things to Think About

1. What do you think causes men to become the types of Tin Men described in this chapter?

2. What are some other types of Tin Men you can think of? How do you think they would describe themselves?

3. How are the Tin Men in this chapter alike? How are they different?

4. Are any of the Tin Men in this chapter better or worse than the others?

5. Do some of the Tin Men in this chapter actually seem to have reasonable ideals that have gotten out of control?

TRY THIS
For Women

Identifying the Tin Men in Your Life
This exercise will create a revealing list that may give you a new perspective on some of the men you've been involved with.
1. Down the left margin of a sheet of notebook paper, list some of the men you've been involved with or dated. You can also add friends and relatives.

2. Next to each name, write down the kind of Tin Man he was. (If he wasn't a Tin Man, just write n/a.)

3. Take a moment to reflect on the results. What did you learn about men in each of those relationships?

TRY THIS
For Men

How Many Tin Men Do You Know?
1. Down the left margin of a sheet of notebook paper, list some of the guys you hang out with and work with. You can also add relatives.

2. Next to each name, write down the type of Tin Man you know them to be. (Write n/a next to the names of guys who you don't think are Tin Men.)

3. Take a moment to reflect on the results. Is your circle of friends and associates mostly Tin Men? How does this influence your beliefs about manhood, sex, and romance?

Chapter 5

MEN VS. WOMEN

It seems that after childhood we should put away the boys-vs.-girls rivalry. But with many men (and women) that doesn't always happen. In fact, many of us continue playing the same games on an adult playing field—one with much higher stakes (children, homes, health, careers, etc.). This is especially true for the Tin Man. For him relationships are power struggles. This inevitably puts him on a collision course with women. Rather than seeing a monogamous, committed relationship or marriage as a goal, he sees it as a thing to be avoided. He views a commitment or marriage as a threat to his freedom and happiness. Especially in the following ways:

The Five Greatest Fears Men Have About Intimacy and Relationships

1. Losing the freedom to pursue other women

This is a huge fear for men who haven't reached the point at which relationships with women are about more than just sex. A man who sees womanizing as a sport, right, or privilege, won't be willing to give up this "freedom" to pursue sex with other women since his sex life is inextricably tied to his view of himself as a "man." After all, isn't a "real man" supposed to spread his seed and prosper?

2. Getting dumped

I once had a conversation with a man at a barber shop that I'll never forget. His wife had just left him for another man and he couldn't understand why. He said that he pampered her like a queen, working a day and night job so she wouldn't have to work. He bought her a new Mustang, a new home, and she had plenty of credit cards. He said he'd sometimes had suspicions that she was cheating on him, but never any solid evidence. Plus, he didn't want to upset her if he was wrong. But one day he came home and had all the evidence he needed. When he walked into the house, the living room and dining room furniture were gone. He looked in the garage, and the Mustang was gone. He looked in the bedroom, and all of her clothes were gone. All she left was a note saying she'd left him for another man.

3. Dragging the ball and chain

Tin Men also believe that relationships exact a huge toll on their wallets. It's a fact that relationships and expenses go hand in hand. For instance, a couple gets married, then buys a new home or apartment, has a baby, upgrades the car to a minivan, etc. Since most Tin Men think it's their responsibility to be the family's sole provider, he fears the bills that come along with such a cycle of events. Even though his significant other may work, this man feels the psychological burden of being the "man" of the house and comes to view his family as a ball and chain.

4. No instruction manual provided

Men love logic. We like instruction manuals, rule books, and guidelines. But feelings aren't logical. And relationships don't come with an instruction manual or a way to test them before using them. To make matters more complicated, they make us feel funny, uncomfortable, unsure of ourselves—and they make us do things we wouldn't ordinarily do. Feelings can send us soaring through the clouds or plunge us into depths we didn't know existed. None of it adds up like a math formula. And Tin Men can't stand the unpredictability or unreliability of it all.

5. Being held emotionally hostage

Some Tin Men see committed relationships as a form of being held hostage. They view it as an automatic loss of freedom, a time when their own thoughts and feelings will be subjected to the control of a woman. Men who think this way believe a man can't really be himself unless he remains single and unattached. Such men support this belief with examples of male friends who have disappeared into relationships and then were permanently missing in action from any activities with the guys. For example, several years ago when I told one of my friends that I was getting married, he said, "Oh well, it's been nice knowing you."

When Tin Men think about all of those things, they convince themselves that bachelorhood is the ideal lifestyle. I'm not saying that there's anything wrong with being single. But bachelorhood Tin Man style isn't about living a peaceful life as a single person. It's about having everything his way, especially relationships with women.

Reaching the Promised Land

The first thing that women must understand is that bachelorhood is sacred to Tin Men. It's the male promised land. Attaining bachelorhood ranks up there with a guy's other great life experiences such as getting his first car, his first sexual experience, turning twenty-one, and graduations. Bachelorhood is a coveted period in a Tin Man's life. Even as a little boy, I fantasized about bachelorhood, back when it meant having a sportscar and being cool. In my teens I added to the fantasy: I wanted a bachelor pad and a little black book filled with the phone numbers of women who would be available to me at the press of a few buttons. Also in the dream was the end of that bachelorhood. Someday, after I'd been inducted to the bachelor hall of fame, I'd settle down with the woman I loved, buy a house, have a couple of kids, and enjoy being a husband and father. I never thought about how I'd make that transition. I just thought it would happen—like flipping a light switch.

The best way to describe what I anticipated from bachelorhood is to compare it to the way girls, even very young girls, fantasize about their wedding day. That's the same romantic vision men have for their bachelorhood. Young girls and boys both hope and dream—but about very different things. Girls dream about commitment, family, and marriage; boys at this stage dream about freedom and being single!

But girls/women are learning they have options. Women today know they can marry and have families, or not get married; they can adopt children instead of worrying about their "biological clock"; and they can be working mothers or homemakers if they so choose. Women are learning to balance it all in one lifetime. In contrast, men are not being offered many new male role models, with the exception of some very progressive men. The changes in the male definition are coming slowly and meeting with strong resistance. That's why the bachelor ideal has remained the same; it's still seen as a girlfest. Many bachelors' lives are big parties in their own honor. Again comes the conflict of men vs. women. The Tin Man views women who come to him in this period of life as trophies or tools to get what he wants. If they want more, he disconnects quickly because he has no intention of ending his bachelor party. On the other hand, the women who want to connect with him wonder why he can't seem to plug in any farther than the bedroom.

But a big change comes as a man nears the end of bachelorhood. Even the most hard-core playboy will grow tired of that lifestyle eventually. While he may feel he is in a safe zone protecting himself from what he sees as the dangers of losing himself to a committed relationship, his own inner desire for real commitment and love will penetrate the wall he's hiding behind sooner or later. Eventually he'll submit to his own desire for more than light casual relationships, no matter how hard he tries to fight it.

But he has a big problem. Though he may want to feel the connection that only comes with a monogamous committed relationship, he fears what such a commitment involves or doesn't even really know what it entails. The bachelor is required to make sacrifices and changes, to live an entirely new life. Starting a new life is frightening to anyone. Imagine moving to a new city with no friends or family. Now add to that the fact that you are in a strange land of foreign tongues where nobody understands what you say and you really don't get what they're saying either. That's how a man feels when he emerges from emotional denial and finds himself face to face with real love and commitment. Sexual conquests are replaced with spiritual bonding. A desire to control and manipulate gives way to sharing thoughts, feelings, and quality time. And most frightening of all, the Tin Man will have to recognize and accept his own vulnerabilities.

The Magic Light Switch

Fast forward. The Tin Man has decided that he wants a whole and committed relationship. He's tired of his old life and has decided that he wants more than a woman in his bed; he wants a woman as part of his life. It's at this point that the Tin Man realizes his emotional numbness has disconnected him from the very feelings he now needs to have in a meaningful relationship. He thought when the time came, he could just flip a switch and be ready for commitment. But now he's discovered that it's not that simple. *There is no magic light switch that will allow the Tin Man to instantly activate his emotions.* But that's what I thought when I was a Tin Man bachelor. However, it doesn't work that way. Instead of finding a magic light switch, he finds nothing but the truth; emotional reconnection will take a learning process because he's been separated from his feelings almost all of his life.

For more on the learning process the Tin Man needs, read the chapters "How the Tin Man Can Change" and "Building the Bridge to Intimacy, One Step at a Time."

The Battle

This is how the battle begins. After the Tin Man has awakened to the fact that he wants a commitment, he realizes that he isn't emotionally ready for it, then he plunges into a battle inside himself. Part of him is drawn to exploring the new uncharted territory of his feelings and emotions, while a bigger part of him is terrified by the thought. Afraid, he falls back into his comfort zone, and resorts to what he knows best—conquering.

Now he starts the power plays. He wants the relationship, but on his terms. He wants to get all of the benefits without having to make a commitment. Tin Men are skilled at getting what they want without giving. They know how to keep relationships right where they want them, whether that means a casual sexual liaison or a long-term relationship that never turns into a wedding ring. Tin Men have three basic strategies for keeping relationships with women right where they want them:

1. Midnight quickies

In this strategy, the Tin Man simply doesn't allow a relationship to get started because he makes himself unavailable other than in the bedroom. If he's pressed for a commitment or a real relationship, he'll disconnect and disappear. Some Tin Men will just lie and tell a woman what he thinks she wants to hear so she will continue to go to bed with him.

Read more about these types of Tin Men in Chapter Four, "Basic Types of Tin Men."

2. Girlfriend for life

The "Girlfriend for life" strategy allows the Tin Man to get all of the benefits of having a steady and dependable relationship without making a formal commitment. In this strategy, the Tin Man takes on the title of "boyfriend" because he knows it comes with special privileges such as always having someone to date, having a special person to spend holidays with, and regular sex. He'll carry the title of boyfriend but he's careful to avoid promises of an engagement or marriage.

3. FALLing in love → *Your marringe*

Since Tin Men desire the benefits of a committed relationship (but don't want to put in the necessary emotional work), some get married without ever really making the real soul-to-soul connection that it takes for a marriage to work. They attempt to be married but are not fully committed emotionally. In other words, they FALL in love. Falling in love means to *Forget About Learning to Love*. These Tin Men attempt to play the role of husband while holding on to the spirit of bachelorhood through affairs on the side. FALLing in love isn't love at all; it's a clumsy stumbling into a relationship. On the other hand, there's rising in love. Rising in love involves two mature people joining forces to create something greater than themselves together.

Though the Tin Man may want to be in love, he's not ready for a serious relationship until he has identified, arrested, and begun to heal from his issues of emotional numbness, conquest, and control. Until he grows out of the old destructive ideas he received about manhood, he is going to continue to see relationships as a battle for control. This is an issue that he must confront and solve for himself. A woman can help, but there's nothing she can do to make him change. See the chapter "A Woman's Touch." For more on the learning process the Tin Man needs, read the chapters "How the Tin Man Can Change" and "Building the Bridge to Intimacy, One Step at a Time."

Unfortunately, some women ignore the fact that they can't

change men and actually see "man saving" and "remodeling" as their job. Such women don't pay attention to the signs along the road that say "turn back, this man isn't ready." Or they just choose to ignore those signs. These women who cling to men are obviously avoiding commitment and they need to address the issues that cause them to do such self-destructive things. For more on this, refer to my book, *Brothers, Lust and Love.*

Things to Think About

1. What things do you and your significant other argue about?

2. Have you been, or are you involved now, in a relationship that you feel is a constant power struggle?

3. Have you ever sustained a relationship with someone who wanted to get serious with you just because it was familiar and comfortable, knowing you had no intentions of taking it farther?

4. What fears do you have about relationships?

5. Are your fears based on your own experiences or things you've seen happen to others in relationships?

6. Have your experiences in relationships reinforced your fears?

7. Have you considered therapy to overcome fears you have of intimacy?

TRY THIS
For Women and Men
Your answers to the following true/false questions will help you evaluate your current relationship or a past one. "True"

responses are clues to things that could possibly cause a power struggle.

1. I have a detailed plan of when and how everything should happen in my relationship.

2. I look forward to arguments with my significant other just for the challenge of it.

3. I must "manage" my significant other because I don't think he/she knows what's best.

4. I believe it is my job to play the role of teacher in the relationship.

5. I'm unquestionably the best qualified to be the decision maker in my relationship.

6. I believe I must keep one up on my significant other to keep him/her from using or manipulating me.

7. I often feel my significant other is trying to tell me what to do.

8. It's within my power to prevent my significant other from cheating on me.

9. It's within my power to create happiness for my significant other.

10. I believe that it is safest to be involved with someone who loves me more than I love him/her.

For more on power struggles, read the chapter " 'Honey, We Need to Talk.' "

Chapter 6

CHECKING FOR VITAL SIGNS: EMOTIONAL NUMBNESS IN MEN

How can a man sleep with several women—and tell each she's the only one?

Why do some men in high positions seem to enjoy intimidating and firing their subordinates?

Why are some men excited by the sight of violence?

Why would a man father children and then walk out on them and their mother?

It's all due to emotional numbness, detachment from feelings. The feelings and emotions of Tin Men are hidden behind a cement wall that was built during boyhood when he first became deluded by a warped idea of manhood: *To be a man you must conquer and control.* To really be an efficient conquering and controlling machine requires a person to become emotionally detached, otherwise one would *feel* the pain of the devastation he caused to others in the process of his conquests; feeling and understanding the pain of others would cause him to stop. But by his understanding of manhood, to stop would mean that he would have conquered nothing, he would not be in control of anything. In his view, that would make him less of a man.

> Reality Check #5: *Personal relationships aren't intended to be battlefields.*

The Tin Man mistakenly views everything as a contest for power and control. He sees his job, relationships, even natural environments as something to be conquered or controlled. But underneath all the bravado, the bad-boy and tough-guy exterior, he's tired of trying to live up to a warped definition of manhood that he can feel is slowly destroying him. He can feel it in his aching body, the tension in his neck, the headaches. His mind is overloaded, always in high gear, spinning even when he's trying to rest. His spirit is restless, wanting to break out of the discomfort of living a lifestyle he knows isn't fulfilling his purpose. He may not act like it on the outside, but he wants a break. And any Tin Man who isn't yet weary from battle is on his way to that inevitable feeling.

In his war, the Tin Man is his own worst enemy. I know because I've been there. I used to work two full-time careers because I was obsessively driven by the conquer and control mentality. At the time I was single and had no children; I didn't need to work two jobs! I should've been enjoying that time. But I thought being a man meant I had to create a fortune. Therefore, during the day I patrolled as a police officer—that job gave me a steady paycheck; at night I worked in my real estate office—that job was to help me get the extra money it would take to buy property and build wealth. In addition to nights, on my off days, I'd work ten hours on real estate. Doing all this, I built up mountains of stress and sought relief. Since my other belief about manhood was that my level of manhood was equal to my ability to seduce women, women became a stress reliever and yet another conquest for me. I didn't drink or smoke, instead I found relief in casual sex with women. I wish I was just an odd case, but for many men, similar patterns of stressful and destructive living are not only normal, but considered manly.

Looking at my past, and the lives of many other men, the issue of emotional numbness is clear. But the real issue here isn't whether or not men have feelings, but how men can learn to access their feelings. *Tin Men aren't devoid of feelings, they're just numb to their feelings.* They believe that connection with too many feelings or too much emotion is weakness, so they close off access to their emotions and feelings; they just don't deal with them. That's why Tin Men are full of so many bottled-up emotions. But if those emotions don't find a constructive release, they'll come to the surface in other ways. This is why so many men turn to sex, drugs, alcohol, eating, or violence. Tin Men don't know that it's okay, even an exercise of personal strength, to connect to their feelings and emotions. Instead, they're concerned about looking strong and in control at all times, even when it's to their detriment. In fact, there are only five situations in which Tin Men feel a display of public emotions is acceptable.

The Five Acceptable Situations in Which Tin Men Can Show Emotion

Although it is never permissible by the Tin Man's rules to totally break down, Tin Men consider it understandable to exhibit their emotions when pushed to the limits of human capacity in the following ways:

1. During war

A battlefield is an acceptable place for men to show a full range of emotions. Amid the horrors of death and destruction, men are pushed to their limits. Under such conditions, it is not uncommon for men to cry, show compassion, courage, leadership, and bravery, and become reflective and philosophical.

2. While playing sports

Let's use the Sunday afternoon football game as an example: You'll see all of the macho rules broken. But that's okay because the Tin Man thinks football players are gladiators. Pro football players put their all on the line in every bone-crunching play. On the field, it's kill or be killed. Football is war. The masculinity of football players is obvious, so they don't have to be self-conscious about some of the on-field traditions that would be considered taboo off the field. Things such as slapping each other on the butt, hugging, jumping on each other in joy, frolicking and dancing together in the end zone, calling each other "baby," and even shedding some tears are done freely on the field. Recently, I've even noticed some football players giving each other "manly" kisses on the cheek.

3. While intoxicated

When a man is drunk or high, it's taken for granted that he's out of control. In this altered state of mind, a man can actually say what he really feels; he can cry, scream, yell, laugh, or do anything else his emotions may possess him to do. He may do many things he wouldn't ordinarily do because his actions are unfiltered by the macho mask. Later, to restore his image, he can make the disclaimer that he was just drunk or high.

4. During a fight

Since fighting is one of the ultimate male proving grounds, extreme displays of emotion while fighting is not really considered unmanly. By the Tin Man's rules, it's okay for a man in a brawl to get so angry that he starts to cry. Tin Men take this to mean that he's just been pushed to his limit and now he's going to really get down and do some serious fighting.

5. *At funerals*

The most stoic of Tin Men will not even cry at the funeral of a close friend or family member. However, many Tin Men will allow themselves to conservatively shed tears at a funeral, but they will almost never be seen crying uncontrollably.

The Tin Man's Numb Relationships with Women

Tin Men are disconnected in their relationships with women in two ways: (1) They see women as *tools* to get something they want (i.e., sex, a place to stay, nurturing, access to a car, money, etc.). Or (2) They see women as *trophies* that show the world their masculinity (i.e., if he can get her, he must be very much a man).

The Tin Man with the "woman-as-a-tool" mentality sees women as objects that perform a specific function. His primary concern isn't a relationship, but what an association with her can do for him. A typical motive is sex, when a man just wants a woman for her body and the power he feels from the thrill of the "conquest."

But some men want more than sex. These men see a particular woman as a way of obtaining a lifestyle they want and make a practice of meeting professional or wealthy women and courting them aggressively until they're involved with them. Such men are status seekers, freeloaders, or con men who are looking for an easy ride. Too lazy to provide for themselves, they seek women who have what they want and then drain them of their resources. These Tin Men will bounce from woman to woman until they find one who will fall for their scheme.

The "woman-as-a-trophy" mentality sees women as a possession, as an achievement. The Tin Man thinks, *What kind of woman can I catch with the skills and tools that I have at my disposal?* This Tin Man is therefore highly likely to seek women who are regarded as beautiful, sexy, high profile, or wealthy. Though some Tin Men are intimidated when a woman earns more money than them or has a high-profile career, this type of Tin Man sees wealthy, high-income, or high-profile women as a challenge. He may not be able to get this type of woman under his financial control, but he feels gaining mental or sexual influence over her is a "victory" that shows evidence of his manhood.

The New and Improved Wife Syndrome

The disconnected relationships of the Tin Man also lead to what I term the "new and improved wife syndrome." Have you ever noticed how so many men dump their original wives after they make it big? Suddenly upon graduation from law school, medical school, or after their career takes off, their original wives, the ones who stood by them and in many cases helped them get going, suddenly aren't pretty enough, young enough, or glamorous enough. Tin Men feel the need to "upgrade" their wives with their new status. Again, in his mind, the woman he has by his side is reflective of his manhood. It's flawed logic, but the Tin Man isn't the most logical creature.

The Tin Man's Numb
Relationships with Men

Too many male relationships simply float on the surface and never get any deeper. This is bad because it keeps us from interacting on a real level where we can get some of the garbage out of our system that is stressing us out. For fear of being looked at as weak, we generally don't tell other guys how we really feel about things. We can't share any emotions or feelings without fear of being ridiculed or called soft or gay.

Instead of addressing such taboo subjects as health, worries, fears, loneliness, feelings about a romantic relationship, etc., our time hanging out with the guys is usually spent talking about sports, women, or our jobs. Those subjects are often the very foundations of our male-male relationships. Guys often become friends just because they work together, they like the same football team, or work out at the same time of day. And that's okay. But we need more intimate connections with each other. Who can understand the thoughts, fears, and triumphs of a guy more than another guy? We neglect a valuable resource for stress relief when we neglect to develop deep and significant friendships with other men.

The Tin Man's Numb Relationships with Children

As Dr. Laura Schlessinger says in *Ten Stupid Things Men Do to Mess Up Their Lives*, ". . . too much of our society's moral and cultural climate has been destructively remiss about fostering and maintaining a sense of male responsibility for investment, involvement and commitment to children."

The problem here is that Tin Men don't see nurturing as a masculine attribute. Tin Men associate nurturing with femininity. They see taking care of children as a job for a woman to do. They believe their primary job is to go out and make money. Though many a Tin Man will help in the nurturing of a child (particularly a baby or an infant) he still feels that it is ultimately the woman's responsibility. Interestingly, there are also some women who don't see nurturing as a masculine attribute.

Here again, the Tin Man remains disconnected. This time, he misses out on an intimate connection with his children. Whether the reason is work, a divorce (with the exception of some men who are prohibited from seeing their children), or he's out cavorting or getting stoned, they miss all of those little moments that mean so much: the first tooth that a child loses, the big game, the first music recital, a big part in the school play, even graduations. I remember watching the biography of a famous multimillionaire entrepreneur on television. When one of his children was interviewed she recalled that her work-obsessed father was not home very much. She cited one example in which her father had to take her to school one morning and didn't even know the name of the school, much less how to get there. Yet our society hails such men as great because of their accomplishments. But are great accomplishments so great if they emotionally disconnect us from our wives and children?

The Tin Man at Work

The Tin Man sees work in the same way he sees his relationships with women: as an ultimate proving ground for his masculinity. But with work it goes a step farther. Many Tin Men don't even have a life outside of their jobs. Their entire world revolves around what they're able to achieve at work. It doesn't matter whether he's a doctor, athlete, lawyer, mechanic, soldier, senator, pilot, scientist, truck driver, or ditch digger, if he's a Tin Man, he sees his work as directly tied to his manhood. He wants to be king of the hill.

As a result, Tin Men are fierce competitors at work. While some appear to be team players, others are radical mavericks who shake things up, but whether they are overt or covert in their methods, all Tin Men believe that a competitive spirit is closely tied to their sense of purpose. They're driven and compulsive about winning and being number one. In this quest to be king of the hill, Tin Men will sacrifice personal relationships, their health, and some will even compromise their values to win. Work is one of the few things Tin Men are openly passionate about. *Tin Men believe a man's work determines his worth.* Take away their work, and most Tin Men wouldn't have a life at all.

The Tin Man Who Defines Manhood Through Physical Power

Frowning face, bulging muscles, fast cars, guns, and vicious dogs are all signs of the type of Tin Man who believes physical power is the only power. This turbo testosterone Tin Man thrives on intimidation and force. He believes that real men slug it out in the streets (or in the home) when they don't agree. He's the kind of guy who stares at people until they look away. The kind of guy who never backs down from a fight. The guy who will get in your face if he doesn't like the way you're looking at him. Unfortunately, he believes all those macho gestures make him a man. *The real truth is that macho antics will eventually get him thrown in jail, injured, or killed.*

All men possess the desire to be physically strong and capable of protecting our families and ourselves, and that's good. But the point at which we go overboard is when we start to believe that our manhood is solely based upon which guy can beat the other guy into the ground with his fist. A good example of this is the male belief that a "real" man will never "back down" from a fight. That's got to be the most stupid thing I've ever heard. First of all, "backing down" is the wrong term altogether. Refusing to fight is seldom actually "backing down"; usually it's more about being smart enough to know that there's nothing to be gained from fighting, with the exception of cases of true defense of self or family. There's never a real winner in a fight because even the supposed winner usually ends up in the hospital, a jail cell, or worse still, six feet under. In the legendary book of military strategy, *The Art of War,* the great military strategist, Sun Tzu, warns us that war (physical confrontation) is costly to both the winner and the loser and is therefore the last, and least desirable method, of solving a dispute. Instead, he first instructs the reader in the many methods there are of defeating one's opponent without ever delivering a blow.

The notion that manhood is based upon physical power is a big delusion and possibly one of the most immediately destructive beliefs of many Tin Men. Manhood is not about physical power. Manhood is about inner power, spiritual strength. Physical strength is temporary; inner power is the only power that actually endures. It's fine to develop biceps, triceps, and pectorals until they burst through your shirt like the Incredible Hulk. But without developing the ability to feel and express emotions in a constructive way, the ability to communicate, and the ability to understand that power and intimidation aren't the definition of manliness, an emphasis on the physical will become a ticket to serious problems.

Things to Think About

1. Why do some men and women believe that men aren't supposed to have deep feelings?

2. In what situations have you seen a grown man cry?

3. As a child, did you ever see a man in your life get emotional? How did it affect you?

4. Do you know any men who are comfortable in expressing their feelings?

TRY THIS
For Women
Take your husband, boyfriend, a male friend, or relative to lunch or dinner. During the course of the dinner or lunch, ask him to tell you about some good memories he has of childhood or teen years. Ask him to tell you about the books, movies, or music he likes. Avoid things that deal with work, money, or any other areas that allow him to put up the macho guard. It will help you understand someone you know (or want to know) a little better. And it will be refreshing for him.

TRY THIS
For Men
Get together with a small group of your male friends for a rap session. Meet at your place or ask one of them if he would like to host. Okay, first of all, you've got to have some food or you're not going to hold the guys' attention very long, so order in a couple of pizzas. Since this is a rap session, not a Super Bowl party, try to have soft drinks, or at least go light on the alcohol. Now you need some discussion topics. Since guys usually need to vent, start there. Here are a few topics a roomful of guys are sure to have some good conversations on: (1) What do I do about the boss/coworker that is really getting on my nerves? (2) Exactly what do women want from us? (3) Do women really want everything to be equal, or just when it's convenient for them? Have a discussion for an hour or so. Joke around and have fun. But avoid allowing the conversation to slip into swapping stories about sex, sports, or cars.

Afterward, turn on the stereo or tune into a game on ESPN just for fun. If everybody has a good time, start doing it on a regular basis.

Chapter 7

TIN MAN JR.: HOW BOYS GROW UP TO BE TIN MEN

Children are born into this world with open minds, eager to freely give and receive love. As adults, we're charged with the huge responsibility of providing children with the love and knowledge they'll need to grow and become all they can be. As an instructor at the Houston Writers-in-the-Schools program, I've had the opportunity to interact with hundreds of elementary and middle school children. Over the years, it has become achingly clear to me just how critical an adult's influence is on a child.

Adults teach children how to live life. To a large extent, young children are exactly what we make them, or more accurately, a reflection of the world around them, a continuation of what they've learned. If they've learned good habits and life skills from their environment, they'll probably repeat them throughout life. If they've learned self-destructive habits from their environment, they will in all likelihood live in a cycle of self-destruction until they learn and establish new patterns and positive habits for themselves. As Dr. Laura Schlessinger says, "History is not destiny."

Daddyhood: Not Just Any Man Will Do!

The *Baltimore Sun* recently reported that over ten million children under eighteen have parents who are divorced or separated. Do boys become Tin Men because there aren't enough fathers living at home to teach them how to be men? At first glance, one might believe that was the entire solution. There's no question that a solid, emotionally balanced male role model is needed for boys. But notice, I said a solid, emotionally balanced role model, not just any person with a Y chromosome.

Any man can be a sperm donor, but being a "daddy" takes a lifetime of care and nurturing. All biological fathers don't deserve the title of "Daddy." Daddy implies caretaker and mentor. Men who casually bring children into the world aren't interested in the child's emotional or physical welfare. Such men routinely avoid child support payments or skip town and abandon their children completely.

On the other hand, the mere presence in the home of a man called "Father" isn't enough if the man isn't a good role model. There are lots of fathers who live right at home with their children, but do little or no daddy work. These are the men who are cold, distant, or even abusive to their children. Some of them do more harm than good to the children they live with.

Home Training

Regardless of whether a boy is raised with a father in the home or by a single mother, the central issue in boys becoming Tin Men is what boys are taught about manhood and masculinity. Our first and most important lessons about manhood come early and clearly from what the adults in our home teach us. In African American tradition, this is what's called "home training." When we were in public and saw kids misbehaving, my mother would say, "Those kids don't have any home training." Such training, or the lack of it, is how our behaviors are corrected, overlooked, or encouraged. We must look at what we're training boys to do.

- Are boys learning that household chores include things other than doing yardwork and putting out the trash?

- Are boys learning to cook and prepare their own meals?
- Are boys allowed to cuss, fight, and break rules just because "boys will be boys"?
- Are boys taught to respect girls and women?
- Are boys told at home that they'd better win any fight they have at school?
- Are boys taught that their self-worth is about more than their strength and speed?
- Are boys learning that academic and artistic pursuits are valid activities for men?
- Are boys learning that playing sports can be enjoyable simply for the sake of a good game?

Of course, it all depends on the home. The balanced male role model in the home represents a full range of manhood for boys. From him, boys learn healthy attributes that are traditionally masculine, but not lacking connection with feelings and emotions. For example, a healthy male role model is a man who encourages a boy to have courage, but teaches him to avoid foolish pride; he instructs a boy in ways to become physically strong, but teaches him his inner strength is his real power; he teaches a boy how to defend himself while explaining that fighting is never the best way to resolve a conflict. And when a boy needs a shoulder to cry on, he doesn't tell him to "stop crying and be a man" because he knows men can have tears, too, even when they don't show them.

But the overly macho male role model places too much emphasis on conquering, controlling, and manipulating. He encourages boys to see masculinity in terms of physical power and the ability to control women. A lazy or derelict role model teaches boys that men have no responsibility to their families; that men can get by just on the fact that they're men. Then there's the absentee father, the one who has skipped out on his family, ignores them, or comes and goes infrequently. Also, as stated earlier, he could actually even be a man who is physically present in the home, but disconnected and distant. This man leaves boys to fend for themselves in discovering the meaning of manhood. These boys will hopefully have a strong mother and encounter positive and balanced male role models in their lives. If not, they may adopt society's Tin Man definition of manhood by default (for definition, see Chapter One, "What's a Tin Man?").

What Boys Are Learning Outside the Home

We would all like to believe that a disciplined childhood, good parental role models, and a hot meal on the table every night would assure that boys would grow up to be loving, sensitive, yet masculine, men. Those things certainly can help, but they aren't an end in themselves. I had a wonderful upbringing, I was fortunate enough to have both parents present in the home, but I didn't grow up in a vacuum.

The world beyond the front door has a great influence on how boys perceive, learn about, and interpret manhood in our society. The images that our society honor, uphold, and celebrate as manly have traditionally involved power, aggression, domination, control, and even ruthlessness. Look at some of the kinds of men we typically regard as manly: athletes, police officers, military men, business tycoons, even gangsters.

TV, MOVIES, RADIO, AND VIDEO GAMES

Have you listened to the lyrics of any popular music lately? Catchy lyrics and flashy music videos celebrate male rappers and rock stars who go on and on about their sexual experiences and abilities; brokenhearted women croon love songs about emotionally unavailable or unfaithful men.

Have you checked out your son's favorite video game lately? I recently watched two fifth graders play a video wrestling game.

The characters were beating the life out of each other and cursing while sound effects of punches and slaps reverberated from the television. When they tired of that game, they popped in another one in which the main character was blasting his way through a dungeon killing more people per second than an entire army. "All right! I got the chain saw now," the younger boy shrieked. He started clicking the joystick and weaving a path of gory destruction. Some shrug and say it's just a game. But I agree with those who say these games desensitize boys to violence; they even glorify violence. And in the wake of the recent rash of school violence, this matter needs to be taken more seriously.

Boys get some of their most enduring beliefs and distortions about manhood from Hollywood movies featuring characters not exactly intended to be the role models they become. Some of the Tin Men found in films today and in the past are: the righteous hell-raiser (*Die Hard*); the ladies' man (James Bond, Agent 007); the ruthless businessman (*Wall Street*); the functional maniac (*Lethal Weapon*); the cold and calculated warrior machine (*Terminator*); the man who will only go out in a blaze of glory (*Billy Jack*); the cool and mighty avenger (*Batman*); the aloof and wise hermit (*The Horse Whisperer*); and the clown (*Rush Hour*).

LITTLE LEAGUE, MORE THAN A GAME

When I was growing up (and I don't think much has changed since then) Little League wasn't just a game, it was an important formal proving ground for manhood, a place where we sharpened and practiced the manly virtues we had learned at home and in society, the virtues we were to live up to. But it wasn't a fair proving ground; it only rewarded speed, strength, agility, aggression, and power. Immediately, those of us who had size or speed began to emerge as leaders among the boys. And since Little League teams were neighborhood based, the leaders on the Little League football, basketball, and baseball teams became the leaders in school and the neighborhood. The pecking order of the neighborhood boys was derived from our prowess on the Little League playing fields.

In Little League, we also learned the importance of hiding our pain. In fact, being injured was a big time to prove your manhood. The unwritten rule was the more pain you could take without tears, the more of a "man" you were. I remember what a coach told one of my football teammates, as the ten-year-old boy was curled up on the ground from having been run over by a boy twice his size: "Get up, boy. Is it going to kill you?" My friend mumbled a "No, sir," and then shakily stood up. "Walk it off," he was told; the sideline remedy for every injury.

My turn to "tough out" an injury came when I was fourteen. In baseball, my position was catcher. Early in a game I stuck my hand out too far while the batter was swinging. The bat struck my hand, cracking a bone and breaking my finger. My coach, a short-tempered man who got high on being macho, showed little sympathy. He told me to "walk it off" and then stuck my finger into a cup of ice. For the rest of the game, I sat on the bench in pain watching my hand swell. That night my mother took me to the doctor and we discovered that I'd broken my finger and a bone in my hand. My mother was furious. She gave my coach an earful and me as well. "Why didn't you tell him your hand was hurting? Why didn't you call home?" she asked.

"I don't know." I shrugged and mumbled. But I did know. I didn't want to look like a "sissy" complaining about an injury. So I thought it was better to suffer in silence.

In addition to holding in physical pain in public, we learned in Little League to hold in our emotional pain, too. Occasionally after a tough loss, some of us would break down and have a good cry. When I was twelve, my team missed the baseball championship by one run scored in the last inning of the game. When that winning run crossed the plate, we somberly marched out to shake the other team's hands, as custom dictated. Then the tears started. Some of us had little traces, some of us had big tears rolling down our cheeks. A few boys were bawling full force. Some of the boys on the other team patted us on the back in sympathy and some laughed at us. Our coach yelled at us to stop crying like sissies! "Get angry, take it out on them next year!" he yelled. What about now? We hurt right then. This was another initiation into the male fraternity, learning how we were supposed to deal with our loss and frustration. That day on the baseball field we learned to hold in our pain, ignore it. And if necessary, to take our anger out on somebody else.

Although some grown men are obsessive about sports, that doesn't overshadow the fact that organized sports is a good thing for boys (and girls). When properly taught and supervised it's an excellent place for boys to learn some valuable lessons about life and manhood in a healthy environment. It teaches the mental accuracy needed for quick and sharp reactions, the importance of physical conditioning, and spiritual growth—cultivating the ability to succeed in the face of adversity. The importance of practice, self-discipline, fair competition, following rules; there's lots to learn about life in organized sports. But the lessons on the field have to be successfully transferred into real life. And that can only happen when the experience of the sport itself is emphasized over a compulsive drive to win at all costs.

LEARNING THE ART OF COOLNESS

School is the formal academy of our training in the male fraternity. It is here that we have many of our most intense social lessons; we have our first big fight, we start to discover girls. School is where we cultivate the art of coolness and nonchalance, another skill high on the list of coveted male traits. We boys quickly realized if you were cool, you were more of a "man." To be cool meant that you were in control, quietly powerful, and implied (eventually) that you were good with the girls.

But when it came to being cool, I was slow at coming out of the gate. Quite frankly, at age thirteen, I wasn't overly interested in being cool. But one day, I realized that I'd better get cool real fast if I was going to survive socially. On a beautiful spring afternoon when I was a seventh grader riding the school bus home, I was excited because I was looking forward to getting home to play with my electric football set. That morning I'd left everything set up and ready to go.

Several rows behind me, a few of the guys were comparing notes on girls. One boy, Jesse, claimed he'd already had sex and all the other guys called him a liar. He began to make his case and then one of his friends shouted, "Jesse hasn't had sex, he still plays with toys. He has a bunch of GI Joes in his room!" Maligned, Jesse tried with no success to argue that point down.

I hunkered down in my seat. I wasn't going to tease him. I still played with toys and I didn't see what the big deal was. For a moment, I wondered if there was something wrong with me. I hadn't had sex and I still played with toys. Was I a man or just a boy? I saw that if I wanted to maintain my cool ranking, the electric football game would have to be underground from then on. It did go underground for a little while, then I turned it off, boxed it up, and put it in the garage.

In a sad way, becoming cool was probably the final blow to any remaining boyhood innocence. From that point, I was officially a Tin Man in training. From that point, my clothes, being a good dancer, getting the phone numbers of girls, and of course, playing football became the public me. But inside, I still wanted to go home and play a game of electric football.

THE LOCKER ROOM

The locker room is where we first learned to speak and decode Tin Speak. We learned that venturing into discussions of academics, literature, art, or subjects heavy with feelings were not tolerated unless they had a macho angle attached. Our conversations were limited to sports, weather, cars, money, and of course, girls.

But the locker room was about more than talking. It was also a place where we learned and passed on very specific male social practices, unwritten rules, and codes that, if violated, would have you thrown out of the male fraternity. For example, in the locker room, where conversations about girls were the norm, we became well versed in the proper way to describe sex with women. It had to be insensitive and detached. Terms such as balling, hitting, slamming, banging, popping, riding, destroying, breaking, crushing, jumping, and killing were the acceptable vocabulary. Those are certainly some garrish ways to describe making love. But those terms reflected the attitudes we were learning. Though some people will say "boys will be boys," it's not that simple, because left unchecked, those attitudes carry over into manhood.

GIRLS, GIRLS, GIRLS

As grade school boys, we thought girls were foreign beings from the planet Cooties, from whom we'd get cooties if we touched them. So we avoided them. But as we hit our teens and our hormones woke up, then erupted, we abandoned the idea that girls were to be avoided. Instead, we were magnetically drawn to them. We were overtaken by the desire to be with girls. Suddenly everything we did centered around girls. We wanted to go to parties, to the mall, even to school—anywhere we could find more girls.

Such interests seemed innocent enough, but under the tutelage of Tin Men and prevailing social attitudes about manhood, our young egos had already taken a strong turn toward the macho. Already we saw girls as tools and trophies. The attractive popular girls such as cheerleaders, homecoming queens, and girls popular for their looks, could make us look good and increase our reputation on campus (trophies). Any girl who was willing to French kiss us behind the gym, let us steal a feel, or go all the way, we saw as a great chance to satisfy our sexual curiosities and put a notch in our belts (tools). Add to this the horrible advice given to us by older Tin Men, and we were well on our way toward a life of misunderstanding with women.

Horrible Advice Tin Men
Give Boys About Women

Some of the things I was told by various Tin Men:

1. Always have two or three girlfriends.
2. Just tell women what they want to hear so you can get sex.
3. Women want you to tell them what to do and "keep them in line."
4. No matter what, get all the sex you can.
5. Never love a girl more than she loves you.

I wish I were only making those things up, but I'm not. There are some adult men in this world who shouldn't have any discussions with boys about relationships because their opinions are too warped. When boys start getting interested in girls and begin to ask questions about women and relationships, they need well-balanced male role models to teach them how to treat women with respect while teaching them to honor themselves as well. Otherwise a boy may make some very bad decisions based on the poor advice he gets from other boys in the locker room, or worse—poor male role models.

Things to Think About

1. What are some things you've told boys about being a man? Have you ever told a boy that it was not manly to express his feelings? For example, not to cry?

2. What were the values of your gender that you learned? Who taught you these lessons?

3. Are there things you were taught about your gender that you now question?

4. Have you reconstructed a new idea of manhood or womanhood based on your own experiences and not popular opinion?

TRY THIS
For Women
Take your daughter, niece, or a young girl needing a role model out for a day. Keep it inexpensive and casual. Go to a place—a park, museum, or the beach—where you and the girl can spend quality time talking. Don't be overly preachy—listen more than you talk. Perhaps you could even arrange for your daughter, niece, or a young girl to visit you at work to see what you do.

TRY THIS
For Men
Take your son, nephew, or a young boy needing a role model out for a day. Keep it inexpensive and casual. Go to a place—a park, museum, or the beach—where you and the boy can spend quality time talking. Don't be overly preachy—listen more than you talk. Perhaps you could

even arrange for your son, nephew, or a young boy to visit you at work to see what you do.

If you want to do more, join a local mentoring group such as Big Brothers and Big Sisters. Also, many churches have mentoring programs. If those options aren't suitable, perhaps you could start your own mentoring group or program. For more information on mentoring, contact the National Mentoring Partnership at (877) 232-6368, or on the Web at *www.mentoring.org*.

Chapter 8

SEX: THE SWEET ILLUSION

"There is a fundamental difference between the male and female imagination. We imagine sex directly and intimacy indirectly, while women imagine intimacy directly and sex indirectly. It is not that men are only interested in sex, but that we have been so conditioned to curtail our natural needs for intimacy that only in sex do we have cultural permission to feel close to another human being. . . . What else would you expect from a gender that has been trained for generations to be warriors and workers and conditioned not to feel or express but to stand and deliver?"

—Sam Keene, *Fire in the Belly*

Let's face it, sex is a good thing. And God wouldn't have made it good if it wasn't intended to be enjoyed. But for Tin Men, intimacy, the most important part of sex, is lost behind the desire for power, control, ego gratification, or addiction. Instead of an ultimate connection, sex for a Tin Man is a selfish endeavor. Instead of making sex an exchange of love and intimacy, Tin Men take their conquering attitude right into the bedroom with them.

Tin Men on Sex

James, age 27, single
Trying to have it all his way.

"I don't want a girlfriend, they're too much trouble and take up too much time. What I prefer to do is have several women. When I want to have sex, I call one of them up, go to her place, and get off a couple of good times. That's all I need . . . and then I'm gone."

As a former Tin Man, I know where James is coming from. I was similar to him in my Tin Man days. He actually wants the company and intimacy of women, but on his own time and terms. Since he wants to be close but not emotionally involved, he keeps himself spread among several women. This way, he doesn't have to become attached to one woman. This allows him to minimize his chances of ever getting hurt or having to connect with a woman other than in the limited emotional way and sexually. If any woman pushes for more, he'll back off and go to the next.

Chris, age 34, single
Addicted to sex?

"I've been in four different beds this week. I have to concentrate, or I'll say the wrong name during orgasm."

Chris said it was simple. He just wanted sex. He admits that he has to have sex several times a week with different women to give him something to feel good about. Two of the women are single, one of which he lies to and tells her she's the only woman in his life. The other has agreed to a "no strings attached" sexual relationship. One of his girlfriends is married. The fourth is his ex-wife. Is Chris addicted to sex? Perhaps it's an idea he should pursue with a therapist.

Carlton, age 25, single
Thinks sex is love.

"When I really like a woman, I want badly to make love to her to show her how I feel."

I've known Carlton for years and I'd describe him as a confused Romeo. He FALLs in love with a new woman every couple of months (see the chapter "Men vs. Women"). Basically, he sees a woman, loves her looks, gets her number and talks to her on the phone once and thinks he's in love. Then he sets out on a mission to have sex with her. He says this is because he wants to show her his "love" for her. After a month or two, his interest will wane in this new woman and he'll be back to the beginning with another.

Reality Check #6: *Love starts from the inside and works outward, while lust only exists on the outside.*

Terry, age 31, married
On a power trip in the bedroom.

"Sex is the best way to get a woman's mind. Hit it good and she's yours."

Terry is on a power trip. For him the bedroom is a place to prove his manhood by doing what he sees as taking control. He went on to describe his sexual practices in details that bordered on being abusive. His tales were full of women in acrobatic positions enduring his hard pelvic thrusting, which he called "busting" it. He grinned and his eyes beamed as he described the moans and sounds he's heard. But were they sounds of pleasure?

Brian, age 41, divorced
Wants the benefits without a commitment.

"I like having a steady woman to go out with. I don't sleep around either. Too many things you can catch today. But I really don't want to get tied down in a really serious relationship."

Brian was a really nice guy, conservatively dressed, very well spoken and calm. That is, until I asked him about commitments. He perked up and explained very rationally why he keeps women at an emotional distance. Just as with Carlton, I saw myself all over in Brian. He's a typically emotionally detached Tin Man. His divorce two years ago left him bitter and shaky about relationships. He says he has girlfriends come and go, but he won't get serious. He finds the relationships are just right when there's sex, but no move toward commitment.

Andre, age 45, married
Cheats on his wife.

"What my wife doesn't know, won't hurt her."

Cheating is selfish, deceptive, and manipulative, and it erodes the core of a relationship. When a person is in a relationship she/he is trusting and making a personal investment in another person. If one partner doesn't reciprocate, the relationship doesn't have all the energy it will need to grow and sustain itself. And this isn't just about sexual cheating, it could be financial, or even psychological—such as adding unbearable stress to a person's life and not caring that it is destroying him/her. Andre is wrong. When it comes to cheating, what his wife doesn't know *does* hurt her. Nothing on the outside may change immediately, but his cheating crumbles the basic core of their relationship.

Reality Check #7: *Cheating is often a symptom of a larger problem in the cheater's life and/or relationship.*

Men Can't Be Monogamous
Because It's Not in Their Genes?

Some would like to explain the sexual beliefs and practices of the Tin Man as just a man thing, male physiology. That we're slaves to our testosterone. Like dogs, we can't help but to act on an urge. While researchers have found links between testosterone and certain typically male behaviors, biology will not ultimately work as an excuse for promiscuous behavior.

Again, this is the old "boys will be boys" attitude; the attitude that permits men to be emotionally detached, promiscuous, and unaccountable for their actions toward others. The attitude that says men can lie, cheat on, and manipulate women. The attitude that says men don't have to control their anger. The attitude that allows men to walk away from their families without responsibility. That's unhealthy and destructive behavior for any human being. It can't be simply overlooked because of what lab results may or may not say. *Lab results don't mend broken hearts and lives.*

The biological maintenance argument is just a big cop-out for men. No matter how much scientific data are accumulated to support a male biological maintenance theory, men are not excused from performing on the most basic level, the human level. A place at which we value love, relationships, and the feelings of others above primal instincts.

If we did everything based on primal instincts, we wouldn't have a functioning civilization. For example, if a man were driving down the road and someone cut him off in traffic and shot the bird at him, he'd pull the other driver over and beat him. If we acted only on primal instincts, when someone had something we wanted, we'd take it. If he made us angry, we'd fight. If we felt threatened in any way, we'd kill. But we all know we have to act in a manner that is safe and to the highest benefit of everyone. Likewise, if we feel a sexual urge, we can't just act on it without realizing there may be consequences to ourselves and others.

Sex and Cheesecake

The consequences of the Tin Man's sexual beliefs and practices can be summed up in an analogy. *Emotionally detached sex is like eating dessert without first eating your meat and vegetables.* And we all know that human beings can't survive by dessert alone. I love cheesecake. But if all I ate was cheesecake, I'd get sick. In fact, most desserts generally have very little or no nutritional value at all. Therefore, the physical body can't thrive or survive on dessert alone. To be in top form, we need nutrients that we can only get through a proper and balanced diet.

Likewise, the mind and spirit can't thrive on an excessive diet of sex that lacks intimacy. Recreational sex, "just for a thrill" sex, "it just happened" sex; it's like eating dessert without eating the meat and vegetables that supply your nutrients. *As we must feed the body good food to make it strong and efficient, we must feed the spirit the emotional nutrients needed to make it stronger.*

Spiritual and emotional nutrients come from activities that connect the mind, body, and soul. Things as simple as turning off the television for some quiet time. Reading inspirational books. Going for a walk. Giving and receiving love in a whole relationship. Prayer that connects you with the creator. Some people also feed their spirits with Tai Chi, Yoga, or meditation. These are all things that move the individual's focus inward. And that's what the Tin Man needs to do to unravel his misunderstanding of sex.

Reality Check #8: *You will not die without sex. But you will perish without love.*

Sexual Addiction, A Serious Issue

When the topic of sexual addiction arises, many people think it's a joke. *But there's nothing funny about sexual addiction; it's real.* Think about it, people use drugs, alcohol, and food to make themselves feel better, change their moods, or cover their emotional pain, so why not sex? In many ways, sex is an ideal drug. It's socially acceptable, it feels good to the mind and body, gives tremendous ego satisfaction, burns calories, erases cares and worries, and gives the sensation of soaring in the clouds. What more could an addict ask for?

But what exactly *is* sexual addiction? Is it the amount of sex a person has? Sexual practices? Number of partners? In his book, *Out of the Shadows: Understanding Sexual Addiction,* Patrick Carnes, Ph.D., suggests some guidelines by which sexually addictive behavior can be detected. He identifies these traits of sexual addiction in his "SAFE" formula. Carnes says, "The question emerges for addicts as to how they determine when their sexual behavior is addictive. The following formula is suggested as a guideline. Signs of compulsive sexuality are when the behavior can be described as follows.

1. It is a *Secret.* Anything that cannot pass public scrutiny will create the shame of a double life.
2. It is *Abusive* to self or others. Anything that is exploitive of or harmful to others or degrades oneself will activate the addictive system.
3. It is used to avoid or is a source of painful *Feelings.* If sexuality is used to alter moods or results in painful mood shifts, it is clearly part of the addictive process.
4. It is *Empty* of a caring, committed relationship. Fundamental to the whole concept of addiction and recovery is the healthy dimension of human

relationships. The addict runs a great risk by being
sexual outside of a committed relationship."

See the resource section of this book for sources that can help
with sexual addiction.

Things to Think About

1. Is sex necessary on a regular basis? Why or why not?

2. Is sex the ultimate act of love and affection to you? Why?

3. Do you think sex creates relationships or relationships
create sex?

4. Do you quickly physically or emotionally pull away from
your partner after sex? If so, why?

5. Do you believe sex is primarily for recreation or intimate
bonding?

TRY THIS
For Women
Find out what a man thinks about sex.

Ask your significant other or some male friends the following questions:
1. How important is sex to you? Why?

2. What do you feel when you're making love to a woman?

3. Is it hard for you to hold and caress a woman after sex?

4. If you had a choice, would you prefer a sexual fling or sex in a relationship? Why?

TRY THIS
For Men
Can you go through a full day without thinking of the women you encounter in public on the train to work, at work, during lunch, in the grocery store, etc. in a sexual way? Try it. If you see a woman you find attractive, just appreciate her beauty without allowing your mind to wander into sexual curiosity. If necessary, say to yourself, *That's a beautiful woman.* But stop your thought there. Don't drift into *I wish I could—* . . . *If I had the chance, I'd—* . . . *I'll bet she can really—* . . . Just don't go there!

Chapter 9

FEMININE TIN SPEAK

There are lots of emotionally balanced, financially stable, and happy women in the world. This chapter is not written about them. This chapter is about women who publicly appear independent, emotionally secure, and stable, but are really looking for a man to come into their lives to rescue them.

Not all women shoot straight about who they are and what they want from relationships. *Not every woman who claims she wants a good man is ready for a good man.* Some women join the chorus and sing the "all the good ones are married, men are all dogs, men only want one thing" blues—yet they don't have it together themselves. When you take away their high caliber careers, impressive degrees, or fabulous looks, some women have no idea who they are. They're no more ready for a relationship than a Tin Man. But most often these are the women who complain the loudest about men, hurling insults at them and finding fault with anything they do.

Reality Check #9: *Some people find that blaming others for their problems is a safe and convenient way to avoid self-improvement.*

It's Not Always the Man's Fault

Women who send mixed messages reinforce the Tin Man's concerns about intimacy. And with good reason, these women are making statements to men that conceal the truth about who they really are. Men who want a commitment are completely turned off by women who send mixed messages. On the other side of the coin, Tin Men, who always run from true and total commitment, find more justification for their fears about relationships from such women because women who send mixed signals are out to trap or dupe men into relationships. Also, another characteristic of women who send mixed signals is that they never stick to what they say. For example, she says, "Cheat and it's over," yet she takes him back time after time. Or she tells a married man, "I don't date married men," yet she goes out with him anyway. *Make no mistake about it, it is a man's fault if he cheats, womanizes, or runs from commitment. However, women who send mixed signals are copartners in that drama.*

Ten Examples of Feminine Tin Speak

1. She says: "I believe the man and woman should share all responsibilities."
Her actions: She acts as though all the responsibilities belong to the man.

Cutting the grass and repairing things around the house is one thing, but when a woman believes everything is the man's job, there's a problem. The woman who makes this statement be-lieves that the man should pay all the bills, solve all the family problems, discipline the kids, solve all of her problems, and be a super lover all night. She may work, but she thinks her money is for herself, the kids, and luxury items. This woman often calls herself an old-fashioned girl, but no matter what she calls it, it's killing her husband.

2. She says: "I don't want to get involved, I just want to go out and have fun."
Her actions: She moves quickly toward a relationship.

This is the kind of woman who has a specific time line in her mind as to how relationships should develop. When she meets a man she likes, she attempts to force her time line on him. She may say she just wants to go out and have fun, but she's on a mission. This type of woman will also typically have a number of preconceived beliefs about dating and a set of rigid rules she believes must be followed. But her relationship rules usually bring about ruin. Then, she rarely looks at what she did to create the situation, only how she feels that yet another man has failed to live up to her "standards."

3. *She says: "I'm looking for a friendship that will lead to commitment."*
Her actions: She seeks the commitment before the friendship.

Unlike the woman who claims she just wants to go out and have fun, this woman is up front about the goal of commitment she desires. But her announcement that she's looking for commitment is often awkward and uncomfortable for any man she's just met because she throws it out on the table like a brick. Right after the guy says "hello," she puts up the "serious inquiries only" sign. She's also quick to analyze, grade, and rate everything he says or does in terms of what kind of husband or mate he will make. But like the woman who says she just wants to go out and have fun, this woman's rigid rules bring about ruin.

4. *She says: "You can trust me with your painful memories of the past."*
Her actions: In arguments, she throws painful things in his face.

This woman finds out what makes a man tick, then she uses those things to control and manipulate him. The things that make him tick that she seeks to find out are childhood experiences, the status of his relationship with his parents, or past relationships. This type of woman is ruthless in her effort to control. When she gets that type of information, she holds on to it until she needs it. Then, when the time comes, she uses it like a sledgehammer, a low blow in an argument.

Mike and Cheryl are an example of this situation.

"Mike, could you talk to your boss about getting Monday off so we can have that three-day weekend at the beach that we've been talking about?"

"Cheryl, you know I can't take off in the middle of a big project like this one."

Cheryl gets angry. "It seems that every project is too big for you to take a break these days."

"Oh, here we go again," Mike snaps as he folds his arms.

"This is why your ex-wife was at another man's house on her back every day after you went to work!"

Ouch!

5. *She says: "I want a good man."*
Her actions: She mistreats all the nice guys.

At different times during my single life, I played both roles, nice guy and guy who didn't give a damn. Guess who got the most women?

It's sad that many men actually believe women don't like nice guys. Of course women will deny that. But that belief didn't just pop out of the sky. Men consistently see some women relentlessly in pursuit of the playboys and bad boys, everything but the nice *men.* Of course, I'm not referring to all women. But those who do think and act this way have told me things such as, "nice guys aren't exciting." Some say nice guys aren't good in bed. Whatever the reason they feel this way, when things explode and the excitement is gone, these women are angry and resentful, often at all men. But go back and look at whom they picked. There's the answer to that problem.

6. *She says: "I just want a midnight quicky."*
Her actions: She really wants a relationship and believes sex will make a man love her.

Men (and women) who believe great sex leads to lasting love are fooling themselves. Great sex leads to orgasm. Orgasms are not relationships, just biological moments. On the other hand, great relationships start outside the bedroom. A great relationship is the result of bonding with another person on a number of significant levels, most important, by discovering the person beneath the physical image we see on the surface. People can get by for a while with the illusion of real bonding in a sexual arrangement. But if they're looking for a real relationship, sex alone will never create a solid foundation.

7. She says: *"I demand monogamy in my marriage (or relationship)."*
Her actions: She doesn't care if he fools around as long as he's discreet.

This is the woman who wants things to look right, even if they're in shambles. She's primarily concerned about stability in her life, keeping things as they are. Her true feelings are that she intends to leave well enough alone. As long as her husband or boyfriend isn't riding around all snuggled up with his girlfriend, seen going in and out of hotel rooms, or having his girlfriends call the house, she's willing to turn her head to his affairs.

8. She says: *"I'm an independent woman. I don't need anything from a man."*
Her actions: She frequently seeks the financial assistance of men she's involved with.

I can't remember how many times I've heard this. It seems to be a standard line in the guidebook for single women. And I don't doubt that many women who say this mean it with all their heart. But there are many women who say those words as a smoke screen, a way not to scare a man off.

For example, when I was single, I remember dating an engineer who was making a good salary, had a well-decorated townhouse, and drove a shiny blue BMW. We talked on the phone lots of times and had gone on a few dates, but we hadn't formed any solid moves toward a real friendship, much less a relationship. That's why I was so shocked when she called me at eight A.M. one Saturday morning sounding desperate. Her car had to be put in the shop for some major repairs and she asked me if she could borrow a thousand dollars. First of all, I didn't have that kind of money, not to mention the fact that I didn't know her well enough to loan it to her. When I said no, she asked if I had an extra car she could borrow. I said, "Extra car?" Again my answer was no. Last, she asked if she could borrow my car for the day. Again I said no. Ironically, this is the same woman who, when I met her, went on and on about how she was so strong and independent and didn't want any money from a man.

She continued to sound desperate, so I asked her a simple and calming question. "Do you know anyone else you can ask?"

"I'll have to call my parents," she said. "But I called you first since we're dating."

9. *She says: "Get out! It's over this time."*
Her actions: She counts the seconds, praying that he will return.

Men know which women mean this and which ones don't. Some women will throw a man out of their lives repeatedly only to take him back out of loneliness, or emotional or financial need. Women who do this are constantly fooling themselves, living in denial about their situations. They may be involved with a cheating man, a freeloader, or even an abusive man.* But time and time again, they find themselves helplessly trapped in situations, some easier than others to disconnect from.

10. *She says: "I'm over my ex."*
Her actions: A. She's constantly angry about him.
               B. She's still having sex with him.

You're not over someone if he constantly occupies a significant amount of your energy. If you're angry every day and living for a moment of revenge, you're not over a person. If you're actively

---

*See the resources section for where to get help when caught in an abusive relationship.

holding a grudge, you're not over someone. If you're depressed, crying, or not eating because of a broken relationship, you're not over that person.

You're certainly not over someone if you're still sleeping with him. Women (and men) who do this often say it's for the convenience. Some even admit that they just can't let go. God only knows how many people have broken up with someone, only to go back and continue a sexual relationship for some time afterward. But that doesn't qualify as some sort of technicality. That's a relationship that is still significantly alive.

Things to Think About

1. Are women who send mixed signals just playing games?

2. Is sending an intentional mixed message a lie, or an acceptable strategy in affairs of the heart?

3. What is the motive of a person who sends mixed signals?

4. What mixed signals do men give to women?

TRY THIS
For Women and Men
   Write down some of the mixed messages you've received.

   Write down some of the mixed messages you've knowingly given.

   Why did you do it? Why do you think others did it to you? Take some time to delve into those ideas, especially as it relates to your own feelings and things you've done. If you keep a journal, this would make a good entry.

Chapter 10

THE TIN WOMAN

Through books, movies, and television talk shows we hear lots more about men fearing feelings and commitment than we do about women with those same problems. I'll be the first to admit that I probably know of more men who avoid intimacy than women. But there are lots of women who have issues about intimacy and are unable to express their true feelings in a meaningful way. This book wouldn't be complete without a discussion about the female parallel to the Tin Man—the Tin Woman. *Like the Tin Man, the Tin Woman fears intimacy, commitments, and/or is disconnected from her own feelings.* Being in a relationship with a Tin Woman can be just as problematic as being involved with a Tin Man.

Contrary to the stereotypes about men, lots of men want to be in committed relationships. But just like women, lots of men who are ready for a deep involvement complain that the women they meet are into playing games or don't seem capable of a commitment, specifically in the following ways:

1. They don't express their feelings.
2. They have difficulty being monogamous.
3. They don't know why they want to be romantically involved with someone else.
4. They're superficial (desiring to be involved with someone else simply for sex, money, or because of their success).

Ironically, such Tin Women invariably seem to be attracted to stable men, just as Tin Men are typically attracted to stable women. And as unbelievable as those relationships are, the only thing that's worse is when a Tin Man and Tin Woman get together. That's the material Jerry Springer shows are made of.

Some Common Types of Tin Women

The Tin Woman's female machismo is usually either passive or aggressive. Some may express desires to be intimate or romantic only through sex. Some Tin Women are obsessed with their work. Some may believe that keeping the balance of power in their favor is a game. There are those women who have little or no regard for the sanctity of marriage or committed relationships and will do anything to get the man they desire. Others may be physically or emotionally abusive or use children as pawns to get what they want. As I mentioned in Chapter One, *women who follow a female version of the macho code are marching right off a cliff behind the Tin Men*. Like Tin Men, Tin Women are self-destructive. Their behavior proves that ultimately, fear of feelings, intimacy, and relationships isn't simply a gender specific issue, it's a human issue.

Some Common Types of Tin Women

This section identifies and explains some of the common types of Tin Women: The Fixer, The Happy "Other Woman," The Gold Digger, Ms. Ego, Daddy Drama, Ms. Ice, The Scorned Woman, The Man-Chasing Mommy, and The Henpecker. These women were introduced in Chapter One. Now let's look at them up close.

THE FIXER

This is the woman who is always busy repairing the lives of other people but doesn't address her own needs. Despite her noble intentions, the Fixer eventually finds herself so weighed down by her support of others that her own life begins to suffer. Fixer women find people or circumstances to attach themselves to that need fixing. She may be involved with a man whom she's trying to rescue. She could be busy trying to repair the lives of her friends and relatives. Or she could be a tireless self-sacrificing matriarch who believes she is not entitled to any pleasures other than the happiness of her family.

THE HAPPY "OTHER WOMAN"

This woman prefers to be involved with married or otherwise committed men. Several women I've known have been in such relationships and they believe the warped notion that being with a married or otherwise committed man provides more security than being with a single man. A woman once told me that at least "you know where he's going after he leaves your house." The inference being that a married man has less time and energy to be promiscuous (that's questionable!) than a single man.

The Happy "Other Woman" is attempting to control her romantic life by sabotaging it. She gets involved with married/committed men because she knows the relationship's boundaries and limitations from the start. She deludes herself into seeing those boundaries as insulation against emotional pain, but after years and years in a superficial relationship—a relationship that's only capable of a limited amount of intimacy—the happy "other woman" realizes she isn't so happy after all.

THE GOLD DIGGER

She needs no introduction. This woman is like a big-game hunter. She's out to conquer men for one thing: money. When she gets what she wants, she leaves the man in ruins and makes her exit.

This woman will give her body and/or the illusion of a relationship in exchange for rent money, lavish vacations, or expensive gifts. Many gold diggers will even go all the way to the altar, and marry men for their money. Such women are prepared to keep up their fake relationships as long as need be, or at least until they jump out of the marriage with a parachute made of gold, i.e., a healthy amount of alimony.

But it would be unfair to say men unwittingly attract gold diggers. Lots of men not only willingly embrace gold diggers, but some men seek them out. They may never verbalize it or be consciously aware of their desire for a gold digger, but their actions communicate that message loud and clear. Every time a man uses his money or material possessions to gain the interest of a woman, he's really saying, "Use me for what I have."

MS. EGO

Ms. Ego is always going off on proud tirades about her status as an independent professional woman. She's quick to say that most men are intimidated by her, can't keep up with her; or that she isn't going to "compromise" for a man who doesn't have more money, status, or formal education than she. And then there's Ms. Ego's favorite line from her theme song: "I don't need a man for anything!" I'd be the first to applaud if that was truly what Ms. Ego meant, but Ms. Ego is in fact very dependent on men. She needs to put men down to build herself up; she's fueled by a wicked sense of superiority.

If she were as independent and self-sufficient as she claims to be, would she have to declare it to everyone all the time? Is the boastful talk a smoke screen for an insecure person who craves male friendships and relationships, but doesn't know how to conduct a relationship based on mutual sharing and interdependence? Just as no Tin Man is an island, neither is the Tin Woman capable of being 100 percent independent of other human relationships.

DADDY DRAMA

This passive Tin Woman is the lost little girl who believes she must have a man in her life to protect and save her. She feels her life is incomplete without a man. The Daddy Drama Tin Woman is looking for security, not necessarily a relationship. An emotional connection isn't as important to her as gaining the sense of security she believes only a man can provide. This woman believes that if a man is anything less than traditionally macho, he isn't manly. She spurns men who don't ooze aggression, power, and control. As a result, she seeks out aggressive and domineering men. But Ms. Daddy Drama soon finds herself stuck in a no-win situation because these types of men are more likely to be abusive or controlling.

MS. ICE

Ms. Ice is cold and ruthless and thinks breaking hearts is fun. Like the Gold Digger, Ms. Ice wants to conquer men. But Ms. Ice is primarily concerned with conquering a man's mind, not his wallet. She uses a variety of methods to do this. The first is the "girl-pal" act—being unassuming and just "hanging out" under the guise of friendship while she's actually making moves for a man's heart all along. She uses this act to gain the trust of men who may be on the rebound from bad relationships. She also uses this act on men who have grown tired of the stale formality that sometimes develops in the dating game. For men who want a girlfriend, Ms. Ice plays boyfriend-girlfriend games until she finally has a man's love, then she manipulates him. When men are only out for sex, Ms. Ice accepts this as a challenge and attempts to "rock their world" under the sheets, purely in the sense of competition.

Usually Ms. Ice just wants the thrill of the conquest. But frequently, her methods are like that of a pirate: After a conquest she'll raid a man for whatever she can get. For example, men who are married to Ms. Ice types are most likely sleeping with the enemy. As one married Ms. Ice told me, "We haven't been having sex as much lately and I'm the kind of woman who wants it all the time. If he doesn't give me what I want, I'm going to go out and do what I've got to do to get it." Another married Ms. Ice said, "I know we're not going to make it in our marriage and I'm just waiting for my husband to try to leave me. I'm not going to cry. I'm just going to take him to court and do everything I can to make him suffer the rest of his life."

THE SCORNED WOMAN

The Scorned Woman has been deeply hurt by a man and she's taking no hostages. She's angry and she's holding every man on Earth responsible. She shoots cross looks at men who meet her glance. She looks upon courteous hellos from men with contempt. Like the Tin Man, the Scorned Woman no longer believes in being vulnerable in a relationship. She says she never wants to be in a relationship again because all men are no-good dogs. Also, she has sour grapes for any woman who's in a relationship. Ladies, if you're bubbling with new love, don't tell her because she'll burst your bubble. If you're happily married, don't share the details with this woman or she'll rain on your parade.

THE MAN-CHASING MOMMY

This woman is convinced that she must have a man in her life at any cost, even at the expense of her children. This is reflected in her lifestyle which is all about using her best energies to attract men. She doesn't take care of the kids and then go out; she goes out and leaves the children to her mother, a relative, or a friend. She's constantly in night clubs, at concerts, ball games, parties, or any other place she thinks she can meet men. She has more social activities than women who don't even have children. Note, I'm not talking about a responsible single mother on a night out; I'm talking about women who are so busy searching for a man that they avoid responsibilities to their own children.

Perhaps it wouldn't be so bad if she were taking care of home first, but she isn't. Her children don't get quality time with their mother because she's more concerned about meeting men than being a mother. Even worse, the Man-Chasing Mommy is constantly bringing new men home to meet her children. Often she's in the living room openly hugging and kissing in front of the kids with a different man on Tuesday night than the one who was over on Thursday. She may understand it all, but the kids don't.

THE HENPECKER

The Henpecker is a Tin Woman who wants to control the man in her life at all costs. She believes if she continuously keeps pressure on him, she can make him act the way she wants him to. She also uses nagging as a weapon. The nagging is usually whining or begging until a man gives in to what she wants. On the other hand, there's the aggressive approach used by some Henpeckers. In this style, she actually attempts to force a man to do what she wants. Her methods include cut-downs, teasing, public tantrums, or breaking things. Some women will even resort to physical attacks to get a man to do what they want.

Things to Think About

1. Do you know any women who fit into the Tin Woman categories?

2. If you do know women who fit into the Tin Woman categories, how have they affected your life?

3. Does society view Tin Women and Tin Men by a different set of rules? If yes, why?

TRY THIS
For Women
Make a list of the Tin Women you know. Label each as the type of Tin Woman she is. Create new categories if necessary. Reflect on each woman.

Do you recognize any of the Tin Woman qualities in yourself?

Do you know why she's a Tin Woman?

Is she working to heal from her self-destructive beliefs and lifestyle?

TRY THIS
For Men
List the categories of Tin Women. Fill in each category with the names of women you know, or have known, who fit into those categories. Create new categories if necessary.

How many Tin Women have been a part of your life?

What influence have they had on your thinking? Your lifestyle?

Chapter 11

MACHO-CIDE: WARNING!
BEING A TIN MAN CAN BE
DANGEROUS TO YOUR HEALTH!

Macho-cide: *Self-destructive male behavior based upon delusions of invulnerability.*

It's no secret. Men hate going to the doctor. We think it makes us look weak. Instead of visiting a doctor when we begin to experience symptoms of health problems, we try to "tough it out." Sometimes, we know in our gut that we're ill but we go into full denial about it. I used to be that way too, until that mentality almost killed me.

How I Almost Committed Macho-cide

Macho-cide, the self-destructive male behavior that is based upon delusions of invulnerability and desire for control, literally destroys men! How many fights have men been injured or killed in because they didn't have the inner strength to walk away instead of fighting? How many men suffer from stress-related problems or emotional pain that is acted out in the form of addictions, rage, or womanizing?

And there's the issue of going to the doctor. As I've said before, I'm not shaking my finger at all the guys out there, I'm a recovering Tin Man myself. I'll be the first to admit that men have a problem with getting medical attention. It springs from the same source as not asking for directions. Both going to the doctor and asking for directions send the same signal: "I need help," and men translate that to mean, "I'm not in control; therefore I'm not a real man." So rather than ask for directions, we circle the freeway looking for an exit that we've passed ten times. It's the same with going to the doctor. We would rather "tough it out" than to admit that we're in need of help or there may be something wrong with us. As I've stated throughout this book, I'm speaking from experience. I used to be afraid to go to the doctor, but then I had an experience that forced me to change.

A couple of summers ago, I came down with a hacking cough. I was sure it was the result of working up a sweat in a gym where the air conditioner blasted cold air to counteract the harsh Houston summer heat. I continued to cough but eventually the cough would not be ignored. It persisted and got worse. Soon my cough was vibrating painfully from deep inside my chest.

But being a Tin Man, I didn't want to miss a day from work or "waste" time going to the doctor. I rationalized that I was just suffering a little infection that I could beat. But the symptoms got worse. My chest started feeling full and heavy. Within a week, I was housebound and unable to walk up and down the stairs without resting. I was also having difficulty taking deep breaths. A few days later my chest felt so congested that I had to sleep sitting upright in a chair to avoid the sensation of suffocating. But I was still determined to tough it out!

Eventually I could only breathe by taking in short gasps of air; I felt like I was drowning. I prayed to avoid feeling panicked. Finally I got the message: Maybe there *was* something wrong with me. At the insistence of my then fiancée (now wife), I conceded that I needed to see a doctor. But I didn't go easily. She made the appointment for me and came over to my house to make sure I'd go.

But even as I sat in the waiting room of a pulmonary specialist awaiting the results of my chest X ray, I held out hope that there wasn't much wrong with me. I remember thinking "this doctor's going to think a big man like me is nuts for coming in here with a little baby infection." But I also wondered the opposite. *What if I am sick, really sick?* Which really translated into, *What if I'm vulnerable, not in control?* I think I feared that more than any possible diagnosis. My mind reeled for a moment. *If I'm really sick, I won't be able to make as much money as I want. If I'm really sick, I won't be able to be a good lover. If I'm really sick, I won't be able to stand up to a fight if I need to. How will I be a man?* The thought of being sick was a worse blow to my ego than my body. Those fears raced through my mind as I sat in the waiting room pretending to read an old copy of *Newsweek*. I was too nervous to read anything.

The doctor invited me into his office with a warm smile. From his demeanor, I relaxed, believing that I was just going to need a shot, or a prescription for some antibiotics and be on my way. But once I was inside, he closed the door and hurriedly placed my X rays on the lighted wall. His smile faded and he began to speak in that measured way doctors use when they want to tell you that you're half-dead. "This is a normal X ray," he said, pointing to an X ray with a darkened area in the middle representing the heart. "This is your X ray," he said, circling the heart on the X ray with his finger. At that moment, my heart stopped, my mouth dropped, my pupils narrowed. It looked as though my heart was the size of a soccer ball. At that moment I learned the meaning of "seeing your life flash before your eyes," because that's exactly what happened. Fearing I had an enlarged heart, he immediately referred me as a top priority emergency to a cardiologist in the building. I went upstairs to the cardiologist, who upon seeing my X rays, threw his entire office into red alert mode. At that point I was having nightmares of my chest being cracked open. Next thing I knew I was having probes glued all over my chest and there were wires everywhere.

Fortunately the EKG and sonogram diagnosed the problem. My heart wasn't enlarged. But I did have another serious problem. I had a dangerous amount of fluid surrounding my heart. This diagnosis explained my slow, laborious breathing, fatigue, and feelings of suffocation. The cardiologist explained to me that this was most likely caused by the spread of my untreated bronchitis. He further explained that my condition was not to be taken lightly because it was potentially life threatening.

The cardiologist gave me two options: strong medication or a surgical procedure to drain the fluid. I chose the less invasive option, the medication. During my next couple of visits to the cardiologist I was happy to see that the medication had indeed drained off the fluid; I wouldn't have to have an operation.

But none of this had to happen. I should've gone to the doctor a long time before my health situation became critical. First, my deep hacking cough should've been a clue. I definitely should've gotten the message when the cough became progressively worse and turned into a heavy feeling in my chest. And there was no question I needed help when I had to sleep sitting up to keep from feeling as though I were suffocating. But my desire to remain invulnerable to illness was so strong that I didn't go to the doctor until I almost died. Instead of a near-death experience, I could have just gotten a prescription for antibiotics to cure the bronchitis and never had such a chilling story to tell.

Heed Warning Signals

Most health problems warn us in advance, but men don't see the signals. Most men don't even schedule an annual checkup we're required to have by our job. We usually don't go to the doctor until we're wheeled into the emergency room or our condition is so bad that we're dead on our feet. But we must learn to become more sensitive to issues regarding our health. We need to pay attention to symptoms and seek treatment before we get really sick or even die. Statistics bear out the proof of why men should take their health issues seriously.

- Prostate cancer will strike 244,000 men this year. (African American men are especially at high risk for prostate cancer.)
- Lung cancer is a leading cause of cancer deaths in males.
- Heart disease claims the lives of twice as many men as women.
- Strokes afflict more men than women and are a leading cause of death in men.
- Testicular cancer is the most common cancer for men ages fifteen to thirty-five. (Testicular cancer is most common in white men.)
- More men die from pneumonia and influenza than women.
- For men ages twenty-five to forty-four, HIV is a leading cause of death.
- Approximately 16 million Americans have diabetes, but only about a third of them know it.

Men also need to broaden their definition of "health." It isn't just about our physical bodies. Health extends to our mental and spiritual lives as well. Macho-cide comes in many forms and the only defense against it is to create a total wellness in one's life. Dr. Andrea Sullivan, one of the nation's leading naturopathic physicians, defines "health" in her book *A Path to Healing*.

"Many people believe wellness is simply an absence of symptoms. But health is more than just a physical condition. It is to be in harmony with oneself, one's environment, and one's God. It means being flexible with and accepting of ourselves and others. It involves ways in which we think about and treat ourselves and others. To be well is to have a consciousness of loving for yourself and others. It is to know that you are worthy of having wealth in the form of good health, loving relationships, and prosperity. Being well means recognizing that you are provided for because you are God's child. Good health is trusting the process of life, knowing that everything is perfect even when we don't like it. Good health is physical and psychological vitality, a passion and enthusiasm that lead to an overall sense of wellness and gratitude for the blessings in life. No matter how negative things may appear, there is gratitude for what is good about life. Usually accompanied by feelings of joy, happiness, and love, good health is absence of dis-ease (a lack of ease or feeling of being ill at ease, which is not always or necessarily the same as *disease*), as well as absence of symptoms. When we are truly well, a few physical symptoms are not enough to make us feel unhealthy or ill. Good health is a right. You are entitled to it."

Tin Man Alert: *If you're having any sort of physical, mental, or spiritual health problem, I strongly urge you to see the appropriate professional.* Your physician can assist you with your physical body, a psychologist or counselor can assist you in sorting through issues or struggles you're dealing with, and your religious facilitator can assist you in getting on your spiritual path. Don't suffer in silence. Get help!

Stress Warning Signals

We men are bad about maintaining our physical health, but our state of affairs with mental health maintenance is far worse. We tend to think of our mental health as an afterthought. It doesn't receive much attention until we crash from mental overload. I think it has much to do with the fact that we live in a world that neglects to realize the importance of things we can't see, hear, taste, smell, or touch. But the unseen mental health problems caused by too much stress often don't manifest themselves in a physical way before they've wreaked havoc on a man's health or caused him to explode in rage. Stress is something we need to pay more attention to before it gets out of hand.

Here are some stress warning signals:

- Irritability
- Depression
- Addictions to alcohol, nicotine, drugs, caffeine, food, sex, etc.
- Anxiety
- Insomnia
- Loss of appetite or overeating
- Upset stomach
- Muscle aches
- Grinding teeth

Adopted from Texas Department of Health Materials.

Spiritual Health Warning Signals

The spirit is the engine of our being. It is our essence. Without it, we would just be thoughtless mounds of physical matter. Our world has a tendency to view things from the outside in. But it is the inside that motivates, creates, and guides us. Therefore, it is the foundation of our health and needs the most attention. In the last two chapters of this book, spiritual reawakening and mainte-nance are discussed.

Here are some warning signs of spiritual ill health:

- Desensitization to the effect of your actions on other people
- Desensitization to the effect of your actions on the animals and the environment
- Belief that mankind is dominant, instead of connected, to the world and universe
- Seeking ultimate fulfillment through physical experiences (drugs, sex, material things)
- Feeling like a victim of your own life
- Feeling isolated and disconnected from the people and world around you

Poor Living Habits

Before I started to recover from my Tin Man lifestyle, I was a poster boy for poor living habits. My diet and nutrition were horrible. Typically, I ate sugary cereal for breakfast, fast food for lunch, and usually fast food for dinner. Some days, I wouldn't have time to eat all day, so on those nights I'd sit down to a pizza in front of the television, eat, and go to bed. I thought dessert was one of the five food groups and the only vitamins I had were from the occasional multivitamins I'd take. When I made time to work out I felt compelled to bench press a million pounds, pick up every weight in the gym, and then ride the exercise bike until the sun came up.

I was often irritable and fatigued. At the time I was managing several careers. I was a full-time police officer and realtor, and a part-time freelance magazine writer. I was in a cycle of self-destruction. I overworked, which made me overeat. Overeating made me work out compulsively in the gym. And though I'm not proud of my behavior, the mental pressures caused me to seek a quick release for the stress, and my chosen method was sex with whomever was my "flavor of the month." During all of that, I experienced short bouts of depression and anxiety. I was a mess; my life was totally out of balance. But what's sad is that from the Tin Man's point of view, I was a portrait of success—single, making good money, driving a convertible, no kids, and plenty of female company.

But looking back, I shudder to think of where I'd be now if I hadn't changed. That's not the good life, it's the self-destructive path. The good life is a life of balance that doesn't create the anxieties, fears, addictions, and compulsions that plague us as Tin Men. To live a balanced life, we have to remove the blocks to optimal health:

POOR EATING HABITS
- Junk foods
- Foods with dangerous chemicals/preservatives
- Too much fat
- Too much sodium
- Too much red meat
- Excessive alcohol consumption
- Starvation/fad diets
- Low vitamin intake from not eating fresh fruits and vegetables
- Not drinking enough water

POOR EXERCISE HABITS
- No exercise of any kind
- Inconsistent exercise
- Improper exercise for our physical condition or age
- Improper form and technique

HIGH STRESS
Life in the fast lane is getting too fast. Every new invention that is supposed to add convenience just speeds up our lives even more. For example, the pager was designed to reach people in cases of

urgent matters or emergencies. But today people will page you for any and every reason. Fax machines were supposed to speed up document transfers to make working time more efficient. They've not only done that, they've also succeeded in bringing more matters to our attention in a day than we can handle. E-mail allows people to drop information on us twenty-four hours a day at the click of a mouse. Cell phones scream and command instant attention. And if all that's not enough, there are services that can link all your communications devices so that anyone who wants anything from you, be it a million-dollar decision or just to tell you to bring home a loaf of bread, can simultaneously call your phone, pager, cell phone, fax machine, and e-mail you with one call. Stress is all around us!

HEALTH AND LONGEVITY

I once overheard a story about a man who ran, exercised, and ate right, but contracted cancer and died. The person telling this story was attempting to justify his hard-living lifestyle of drinking and womanizing. I've also heard a similar anecdote about smokers in which a smoker is told to stop smoking or his life would be shortened. The smoker responds, "We've all got to die one day," and takes another drag from his cigarette. Actually both the smoker and the drinking womanizer are right about one thing: We will all have to transcend this life one day. But in both cases, the real point is being missed. Good health is for living better today, not for living longer. Good health habits don't prevent life from taking its normal course, nor does it preclude unpredictable accidents or prevent all illnesses. But it does make the moment better. After all, we don't live in the past or future. What matters most is right now. *Live a healthy lifestyle to increase the quality of your life today, not just the quantity of your years.*

Things to Think About

1. When was my last physical?

2. Have I been ignoring any lingering symptoms?

3. Ladies, have you examined your breasts lately? Men, have you examined your testicles lately?

4. Am I aware of diseases or conditions that are hereditary in my family?

5. Am I aware of diseases or conditions that are typically found in my culture?

6. Have I had the appropriate exam for someone my age?

7. Do I make regular visits to the dentist? Other specialists, such as optometrists?

8. What changes can I make to enhance my health?

9. What am I doing for stress reduction?

10. What strides have I made toward creating inner peace?

TRY THIS
For Women and Men
- Select a physician, go have a checkup.
- Schedule your medical appointments (e.g., internist, dentist, ophthalmologist, etc.) for the upcoming year.
- Commit to regular checkups with your dentist.
- Men, get a prostate exam.
- Women, schedule a mammogram and Pap test.

- If you feel the need, go to a psychiatrist, psychologist, counselor, or pastor and "dump" your feelings. Don't be afraid to schedule as many therapy sessions as needed to work out your problems.
- Start an exercise program or revise your existing exercise program. Focus on moderation and consistency.
- Practice preventive health care. Visit a naturopathic doctor.
- Develop a hobby and do it on a regular basis.
- Turn off the TV and radio to read a book or magazine.
- Schedule a personal day. Take off from work and do nothing at all, no errands, no bills, etc.

Chapter 12

How the Tin Man
Can Change

I took note of something the Rev. Howard Caesar of the Unity Christian Church in Houston, Texas, said in one of his sermons. He related a story about a man on a camping trip who was told not to touch a hot pot that was on a fire. But the man touched it anyway and got burned and dropped the pot. The physical sensation of pain caused the man to immediately disconnect himself from the action that was causing the pain. But isn't it curious, Rev. Caesar observed, that we don't always make that same connection when it comes to mental and spiritual pain?

Often, we hold on to destructive behavior simply because we can't immediately see how it affects us and the people in our lives. But just as the hot pot burned the camper's hand, self-destructive beliefs about manhood threaten to ruin many men. Sadly, many of us don't change our lives until we are drafted by life (see section below) or until we are forced to change. But there is another choice: We can decide to change, alter, and improve our lives. But that's a decision each man must make for himself. However, regardless of whether he wakes up and changes himself or he waits until he crashes into a brick wall, change will come. Change isn't easy, but it's necessary and inevitable.

The Big Four

Up until now, this book has discussed the mind-set of the Tin Man and the history that twisted his mind into seeing everything from work to personal relationships as a battle for conquest and control. But now, knowing the predicament of the Tin Man, we turn our focus to the most important issue, how the Tin Man can change. First, we must identify exactly what he needs to change. Basically, there are four areas the Tin Man must address in order to put his life into a healthy balance.

1. Attitudes and beliefs about sex

The Tin Man believes sex is a conquest of power and control. This attitude causes him to be emotionally numb to women, seeing them as objects rather than people. It also leads him to be prone to promiscuous behavior and seeing sex as "scoring" in a contest of masculinity.

2. Attitude toward work

The Tin Man believes his job is an ultimate proving ground for his manhood. As a supervisor, he may be tyrannical and push others to exhaustion with his compulsive drive to win. As a subordinate, he is driven by ambitions that disconnect him from his own feelings about others and cause him to be insensitive in his personal relationships.

3. Health maintenance

The Tin Man ignores warning signs about his health because he can't acknowledge he's ill or he needs help. The Tin Man thinks he can "tough out" illness and injury, "snap out of" a depression, and ignore his addictions. As a result of ignoring health warning signs (as well as avoiding regular health checkups), the Tin Man puts his physical health and the lives of all who depend on him in a dangerous lack of balance.

4. Beliefs about aggression as manhood

Many Tin Men believe true manhood is only shown through physical aggression. These men believe that everything comes down to who can knock the other guy down first, with a fist, a knife, or gun. They also thrive on intimidation and threats of violence.

The *Dis*-Comfort Zone

One wonders, if the Tin Man knows he's destroying himself, why doesn't he just change? But think about it, positive change is often challenged by difficult or complex circumstances. Have you ever seen someone stay in a relationship that was completely detrimental to their well-being? Do you know people who hate their job, boss, and coworkers? Can you think of anyone you know whose lives are the same mundane routine day after day? I'm sure you can think of several people who fit one or all of those situations, perhaps it is even you.

Everyone at one point or another has slipped into what I call the *dis*-comfort zone: a routine of nongrowth that a person tolerates because it is familiar and appears to be safe. Yet, deep inside we know such zones aren't doing anything to enhance our lives at all.

Basically, it all comes down to fear. We fear life outside of our *dis*-comfort zones. We figure that although we're not necessarily happy, at least we're settled—we know what to expect, even if it's hell. So, we figure, why take a chance on something new that may or may not work out? That's why we tend to stay in a relationship that's smothering us or to keep a job that literally makes us sick. What's most saddening is that in the meantime we're dreaming about a new, more fulfilling life as though it's an abstraction that we can't make real. But we *can* make it real. First, we have to get out of our own way. Some of us will welcome change, some will kick and scream. But one thing is for sure, whether for better or worse, change is inevitable.

Volunteer or Be Drafted

No matter how long we try to remain in our *dis*-comfort zones, ultimately we will be forced to change. That change comes in two ways. One is a voluntary change; a man takes a look at his life and realizes that if he doesn't change, he'll ruin himself and/or those who love him. The other is being drafted, the less appealing of the two choices. This is when you've continued to ignore the call to change and life comes to teach you a hard lesson. Unfortunately, many of us just don't get it until we get knocked on our behinds. For the Tin Man, that translates into: being caught cheating; having a heart attack; getting high blood pressure; going to prison on a DWI conviction (or worse, causing a deadly accident); killing someone in an act of rage; or making a fortune then feeling desperately guilty about all the treachery we committed in the process.

It doesn't have to be that way. It's much better to volunteer than to be drafted. Ever wonder why the same thing keeps happening to you over and over? When this happens to us, we don't have bad luck, we're just not getting the lesson. Until we accept our mistakes and make attempts to correct them, the lessons will continue to repeat themselves until they are learned once and for all.

Time to Do Some Homework

"Homework?" you ask. Homework is the inner work we have to do to make ourselves whole beings, to find peace within, to feel at home in our skin. One day before one of my workshops, I was talking about focusing on our problems, and a woman in the group said, "I know all that, but it's just too hard. I'd rather keep blaming other people for my problems."

But the solutions to our issues will not come from blaming others. Certainly, our relations with others must be examined when figuring ourselves out. But ultimately blaming doesn't advance our agenda at all. For example, we Tin Men could attempt to point to social conditioning as the reason we are so focused on power and control. Although there's much truth to that, it doesn't solve the issue of how we can halt our self-destructive lifestyles. And that's the major point: How do we save ourselves from ourselves? That's where homework comes in.

Homework starts with a very small step—the realization that you're in a lifestyle that is not good for you. It requires an admission that you aren't happy with your life as it is. To do homework you need the courage to be honest with yourself—to admit that you are just a man. Then you can move on to get the help you need (be it mental, physical, spiritual, or all three). Homework is the place we turn the corner in our lives. The place we make the move that will break the cycle.

Reality Check #10: *A person must want to change before anyone can help him or her.*

Why Is Getting Spiritual Necessary?

The evidence that proves we need a spiritual base is all around us. We try all sorts of things to fill the voids in our lives, but they never seem to work. We have dreams, but when fulfilled, they leave us wanting more. We try cars and homes, but then we get what we want only to discover that we want something more luxurious. We try sensual solutions—sex, eating, drinking, or drugs—but those things never satisfy us either. Even in our careers, we work hard to achieve our goals, only to say, *Now what? What's next? Is this all there is? I sacrificed everything for this?*

Sometimes when extreme measures have failed, we discover

that it's time to look within, get quiet, and listen to ourselves. It's the knocking we've heard at the door, the voice we hear, the feeling we have that tells us there's a better path for life. The spirit is saying it needs to be charged up; it's calling for a connection with the ultimate power source.

> *"Reflection, evaluation, and unlearning*
> *require a willingness to do the grunge work."*
> —Iyanla Vanzant

Asking for God's Help

In asking for God's help, I'm not suggesting a mindless mumbling of words or the robotic following of rites and rituals. *Asking for God's help is to seek a oneness with the unlimited power and energy of the creator; a source we are heir to by human birthright.* But accessing that power must begin with humility of heart and understanding that our way, the man as a demigod way, has failed our families, our nations, our planet, and us as men. We have to begin with the admission that we need help.

Such an admission is a release of our desire to be in control. To become more powerful, we must first admit that we aren't the all powerful. That admission removes the blocks that keep us from forming strong interdependent relationships with women and other men. We have to relinquish the need to maintain ultimate control. It takes more courage to do that than it does to spend our entire lives wrestling with everything and everybody in an attempt to have control. The Serenity Prayer offers us a gentle, but powerful reminder.

The Serenity Prayer

God grant me serenity to accept the things I cannot change,
courage to change the things I can,
and wisdom to know the difference.
—*Reinhold Niebuhr*

Reality Check #11: *Release equals peace.*

Should You Seek Therapy?

First of all, there's absolutely nothing wrong with going to therapy. There's nothing unmanly about wanting to sort out the pressures, fears, or struggles you've been grappling with. In fact, going to therapy is a lot smarter than letting things build up until they manifest as a physical illness or you blow your top in a way that gets you or someone else hurt or killed. *You don't have to handle all your problems on your own.* How about this: You *can't* handle all your problems on your own (and you shouldn't want to either).

Most men aren't comfortable with therapy because it involves an admission that they need help. Instead, some would rather talk with friends or family. And that's fine in many situations. But remember that friends and relatives often have a bias. Sometimes they can be too familiar with you or your situation to be objective. Furthermore, all of us have some feelings or emotions that we would feel much more comfortable telling a professional paid to listen to us rather than an unskilled friend or relative.

Visiting a therapist is a constructive way to "dump" some feelings or work out some issues over a period of time. Just be mindful that a therapist isn't going to save you from yourself. You'll have to do that for yourself. However, a competent therapist can be a great facilitator in your healing process.

Today, there are lots of options: You can see either a psychiatrist or psychologist, a pastoral counselor, a minister, or social worker.

Here are some things to keep in mind when choosing a therapist:

- Consider the therapist's educational and professional credentials.
- How much experience does the therapist have?
- Will your insurance cover your sessions? Is flexible payment or sliding scale accepted?
- Is this therapist sensitive to issues of your gender?
- Is this therapist understanding of your ethnic/cultural background?
- Is this therapist sensitive to your religious beliefs?

Things to Think About

1. Do you have any *dis*-comfort zones in your life?

2. Have most of the changes in your life come on a voluntary basis or from being "drafted"?

3. Are you doing the "homework" necessary to make your life what you know it should be? Each of us has different "homework." But here are a few issues in the category of "homework": making amends with someone you've hurt, forgiving someone who has hurt you, releasing anger and bitterness you have against another person, confronting an addiction, coming to terms with a painful experience from your past, releasing the idea that you have to have control over a person or situation in order to feel comfortable.

TRY THIS
For Women and Men

Disconnecting from Your Dis-Comfort Zone
Many of the habits and preferences we have work together
to form a mental safety zone around us. This is especially
true in relationships. We tend to visualize a certain type of
person whom we believe is the right mate for us. This isn't
such a bad idea if the image is based on things such as in-
tegrity and honesty. However, many men and women base
their idea of who their ideal mate is upon superficial criteria
such as income, level of education, status, or physical ap-
pearance.

But safety zones, no matter how safe, secure, and warm
we perceive them to be, hinder our personal growth. In relationships, safety zones can be particularly harmful because
they prevent us from experiencing new people and what
they may be able to share with us. Breaking out of your
safety zone is a way to meet new people. It's also a way to
get more out of life. But you start slowly. The following
seven suggestions can give you practice in stepping outside
of your usual routine:

1. Take a new route home from work or school.
This is one of the easiest ways to break a routine. Go home
a different way; drive down a few different streets in your
neighborhood; or circle the block before pulling into your
driveway.

2. Have lunch with a different person or group.
You will expand your group of associates. You may even
make a new friend. But even if you don't enjoy meeting a
new colleague, at least you had a new experience.

3. Try a new food.
Experiment with new foods, especially ethnic cuisines. Ethnic foods are a great way to learn and appreciate the history and culture of other people.

4. Listen to a different radio station.
For example, if you love R&B, tune in to an easy listening station for a few minutes. If you're a jazz aficionado, tune in to a classical station for a while.

5. See a different kind of movie / television show.
Movies and television provide an easy way by which to experience new thoughts and ideas. Vary your movie/television schedule to include drama, educational, action/adventure, suspense, documentary, comedy, etc. Or skip the movies or television altogether and check out a live performance and enjoy the pulse of live music or theater.

6. Shop in a different mall / store.
Go to that new store near you. Experience the energy of a different place.

7. Vary your reading material.
If you usually read romances, try a nonfiction book. If you usually read nonfiction, dip into a novel instead.

Chapter 13

A Woman's Touch

There are two ways in which women can significantly influence the Tin Man in his views on life and women. The first has to do with how boys are raised. The second has to do with how adult men and women interact with each other. Let's look at those points in detail.

Women and Boys

Boys learn a lot from women. In fact, in the early years of their lives, boys are mostly in contact with women. Some little boys stay at home with their mothers or a baby-sitter until they're old enough to go to school. Later, in preschool, kindergarten, and many of the elementary grades, boys still don't see many men. I've worked with students at elementary schools at which I was one of only three men on the entire campus! And with 10 million fatherless homes in this country, women are often the only parental role model available to young boys.

But what are these boys learning from the women in their lives? Some are getting lots of good lessons about manhood, some aren't. This is because much of what boys learn from women about manhood is based directly on what those women believe manhood to be. For example, a woman who believes that a real man is both masculine and sensitive will guide her son through life's challenges in a way that will allow him to experience a full range of emotions. If her son were afraid of a bully at school, she would reassure him that to fear an aggressive person larger and stronger than him was normal. But she'd also use that opportunity to teach him that he usually has several ways to resolve a problem other than fighting; but if he's in real danger of being harmed, he should defend himself and report the incident immediately to a teacher. (Of course she should visit the school and bring this matter to the boy's teacher and principal immediately.) In contrast, a woman who believes men must be macho robots would teach her son to see a bully as a challenge to his masculinity. She'd tell her son, "If you have a fight at school and you don't win, I'm going to beat you for losing." Fortunately, my parents didn't tell me that. But I clearly remember several boys from the neighborhood saying that was the rule in their homes.

If a boy sees his mother interacting with men in positive ways instead of being demoralized or berated, he will learn to see this as the way men and women interact. His view of male-female interaction will be one of mutual respect and honor. But if he only sees his mother desperately attempting to get a man in her life, he may grow up to believe that women are weak and will do anything for a man's attention. Or if he grows up seeing his mother go off to work while an able-bodied father lies on the couch watching television all day, what effect will that have on him?

Also, as discussed in the chapter "Tin Man Jr.: How Boys Grow Up to Be Tin Men," boys learn different skills from men and women. Some people contend that boys raised only by women don't get all the training they need for life. Although I believe male role models play a critical role in the development of both boys and girls, when necessary, women can raise boys alone by being a good *human* role model. For example, displaying characteristics such as honesty, strength of character, a good work ethic, wisdom, and fairness can be done by any person regardless of gender. Again, it isn't as important to have a man in the house as it is to have the right man in the house.

Consider what pitcher David Wells (at the time a New York Yankee) said to a *Newsweek* reporter after throwing a perfect game, "I dedicate the game to my mother, Ann. She was a fighter like me. They say like mother, like daughter. Well, in this case, it might be like mother, like son."

For more on this subject, see the chapter "Tin Man Jr.: How Boys Grow Up to Be Tin Men."

Mama's Little Man

While we're on the subject of mothers and their sons, I want to raise another important issue. Sometimes when the man of the house is absent or not fulfilling the traditional role of father or husband, the eldest (or only) son is given that role. Unwittingly, the boy becomes the little man of the house, expected to fulfill the role of father, parent, even stand in as a husband in some ways. I'm not a therapist and I don't want to get into the Oedipal implications. But it's certainly interesting food for thought.

For some boys, this man-of-the-house role means taking on the physical chores necessary to run the household. That may be as simple as putting out the garbage on Tuesdays and Thursdays and cutting the grass. For a boy on a farm or ranch, the scope of duties could be larger, such as planting and harvesting a crop or raising cattle.

The man-of-the-house duties also include the roles of protector for some boys; guarding his mother and other children in the home from harm. For example, a boy living in a tough inner-city housing project will feel he has to protect his family from a variety of criminals. And sometimes boys play the role of protector inside the home, too. When I was a teen I knew a guy who had to fight his father to prevent physical abuse of his mother and little brothers.

In addition, some boys have the responsibility of helping to generate income for their families when the father is absent or unable to do so. They will work a job after school. In some cases they drop out of school to work full-time. Though we see them as noble young men, this burden no doubt places a heavy load on their lives.

Probably the heaviest burden to bear for a young boy forced into the role of man-of-the-house is the emotional weight he must carry. Sometimes the mother sets out to make him the man the father wasn't. Or she may emotionally cling to him because the father is emotionally distant, neglectful, or abusive. It becomes a heavy burden for a young boy to feel that he is responsible for an adult; after all, he's still a child. For boys who grow up having to fill this demanding role, it's easy to understand why they'd have the "I have to carry the world on my shoulders" blues of the Tin Man.

What Will Women Tolerate?

Now we turn the subject to women and grown men.

The types of men who don't have good intentions in a relationship will do anything they can get away with. And if one woman won't tolerate their behavior, they'll go to the next because they realize that the numbers are on their side. Too many women are willing to compromise for any part of a man they can get in order to have a man in their lives. Since they know they can always find women who will accept their behavior, they don't change, at least until something forces them to. These are the women such as the Happy "Other Woman," the Daddy Drama, and the Man-Chasing Mommy mentioned in "The Tin Woman" chapter.

Specific behaviors some women tolerate from Tin Men are:

- Lying
- Cheating
- Public humiliation or embarrassing scenes in public

- Never calling when running late for a date
- Only being able to date or spend time when he wants to have sex
- Frequently canceling dates at the last minute or standing her up
- Borrowing money without repayment
- Not helping with household chores ▬▬
- Yelling and threatening behavior
- Physical or mental abuse*

Reality Check #12: *Tolerating unacceptable behavior isn't love.*

On the other hand, there are women who will not tolerate poor behavior from men in relationships. These are women who know they are valuable people worthy of having a good relationship. *Not tolerating poor behavior all starts with seeing yourself as a complete and whole person—that includes married people, too!* A complete and whole person is a person who has discovered that her own personal fulfillment is something she must create for herself. Whole people know that another person isn't a magical all-in-one answer to their dreams, desires, or needs. Of course, complete people, whether married or complete singles, enjoy the idea of having a talented, intelligent, and sexy mate; but *complete people aren't dying of neediness, for them life is going on, and it's goin' on good.*

Reality Check #13: *When two half people get together, they make one whole mess.*

*Abuse in a relationship should never be tolerated. If you're suffering abuse, seek help immediately. The toll-free number, Web site, and TTY of the National Domestic Violence Hotline are listed on the resource list at the back of the book.

Some Women Don't Know Any Better

Like the Tin Man, some women have learned a pattern of relationship interaction with the opposite sex that hinges on behaviors that may feel familiar but certainly aren't good for them. I'm
aware that all of the talk in this book about men and their feelings
isn't going to be accepted by all women. Some women depend on
men being Tin Men; it's part of what makes them feel feminine.
For some women, if their Tin Man were to change and become a
complete man who is unafraid of emotion and is open to intimacy, they wouldn't know what to do. I don't think this is the
majority of women. But there are definitely women who are dependent on men who maintain their traditional male "I've got to
carry the world on my shoulders" role.

I can't give women advice on how to be women. But I can tell
you the way it looks from my side of the fence as a man. Many
women may have grown up watching their mothers and other
women in their circle of influence living in compromised relationships with men. They may have watched their mothers en-
dure emotional abuse and still cling desperately to their men.
Some women had fathers walk out on the family, or witnessed or
experienced physical abuse. There are many factors that could
make young girls distrustful, emotionally numb, or even fearful
of relationships with men. But it could also be the result of her
own romantic experiences as a young woman. She may have
started off open-minded and trusting only to fall prey to men who
saw such traits as an opportunity to exploit her for whatever he
wanted.

As I look at this situation from my side of the fence, it seems
that these women become locked into a pattern in which they expect all men to act in the same way as the poor examples they've
known. Inevitably this leads to heartbreak after heartbreak. But
they continue to choose the same unhealthy mates. They don't
seem to be attracted to men who don't "live down" to their ex-

pectations. But when a woman is caught in this type of cycle, she's bringing herself grief and she needs to break out of it. That's when it's time to see a therapist to work through some of the issues that are causing her to make poor choices in mates. For more, see "The Tin Woman" and "Feminine Tin Speak."

You Can't Change Him

I've said it before in an entire chapter in *Brothers, Lust and Love* and I'll say it again now, it's that important. *Women can't change men. Men have to change themselves.* And in cases in which men don't want to change, women have two options: Remove themselves from the relationship; or remain in the bad relationship, in which case they're participating in the creation of their own hell. There are no ifs, ands, or buts about it. I know women who live in hellish relationships day after day. I also know women who've escaped such relationships, in some situations, packing up the kids, getting an apartment, filing for child support, and starting life all over.

But it often takes some learning for some women to realize that their love alone can't sustain a relationship, that they aren't super-nurturers. Or to accept that a relationship isn't going to get better and that it's unraveling her piece by piece. This is when many women I've talked to start getting teary and say, "But I love him . . ." usually followed by a discourse of wondering why the man she loves can't just see that. But living in a relationship that is 365 days of hell isn't going to change anything for him or you.

You Can't Change Him, But There
Are Some Things You Can Do to
Help Him Change Himself

1. Don't try to be a super-nurturer.

You can't simply love a man so much that he'll change, especially a Tin Man. If you bend over backward for him, he'll surely accept your sympathy and good treatment, but he may not return it to you because a Tin Man is in a self-centered mode of living. I'm not saying to be insensitive and cold, just don't fool yourself about the reality of the situation—the issues he faces are out of your control.

Reality Check #14: *Don't play the role of parent in your relationship.*

2. Don't try to repair his past.

You can't repair his past. Let me say that again: *You can't repair his past!* True enough, he may be drowning daily in a world of his troubles. It could be memories of bad relationships, traumatic childhood experiences, or rebuilding himself after being in jail or struggling with chemical dependency. But you can't sort out the people and events from his past for him. If he has deeply rooted wounds or ghosts to confront, perhaps he should see a therapist to help him begin the process of healing.

3. Don't make excuses for poor behavior.

Denial is not the path to bliss. Closing your eyes and sticking your head in the sand does not repair broken relationships or correct poor behavior. What that does is cause the situation to escalate to a crisis point at which things can no longer be ignored. As I've already stated in this book, the old "boys will be boys" excuse isn't going to fly. That's only a poor bandage for a gaping problem. Even if your friends, or your own mother, tell you to look the other way when you're being treated unfairly, don't do it. If you start making excuses today, you'll have to lie to yourself more and more as things continue to get worse.

4. Don't compromise your health and well-being.

Relationships with some Tin Men pose an immediate threat to a woman's health and well-being because of the lifestyle he leads (and may want her to participate in). Don't ever resort to drug abuse, heavy drinking, unsafe or undesirable sexual practices, participation in illegal activities, or any other lessening of your beliefs, values, or morals in order to keep a man in your life. *Your first and most important relationship is with yourself.* You are precious and sacred and must allow no person, man or woman, to violate that.

5. Insist on monogamy.

This is nonnegotiable: There must be monogamy in a relationship. No "boys will be boys" excuse will cover for this. Since the Tin Man is afraid of his feelings and relationships he will never be successful in a relationship if he doesn't learn to be monogamous. Monogamy, for the Tin Man, is a frightening prospect because he has to focus on one relationship. This often gives him the feeling that he's missing out on the other women out there. But if that's how he feels, his state of mind isn't right for a commitment.

6. Don't blame the other woman.

If you discover your husband or boyfriend is cheating, it's easy to focus your anger on the other woman. It's easy to see her as an invader who is attempting to take what is yours. But instead, you have to consider the facts of the matter. Treat the problem, not the symptom. She's just a vehicle by which the problem is manifested. *Your real issue is with your husband or boyfriend.* He's the person who has the commitment to you. He's the one who violated your trust and broke the bond you had. I'm certainly not making the implication that she is guiltless if she knowingly participated in your mate's cheating on you—in that case, she's wrong, too. But your focus should be on your husband/boyfriend and resolving the situation with him.

7. Don't be needy.

Needy women believe they must have a man in their lives or they will curl up and die. That's why Tin Men love to find women who have that neediness. They're so desperate that all they want is a little attention or affection and in return they'll give anything or do anything. They don't insist on much time together. They don't care if they're not the only woman in his life. They're always willing to be last on the list of things to do. And they're afraid to ask him to make an emotional connection or commitment because they know he'll leave them. They just take what they can get. Obviously, they make the Tin Man worse.

8. Never overlook abuse.

Psychologists, social workers, and the law enforcement community warn us that spousal abuse isn't something that can ever be overlooked or viewed as an isolated event. Abuse happens in a cycle in which basically a dangerous escalation occurs. For example, it may start with verbal threats and over a period of time (or quickly) degrade to shoving and kicking, choking, punching, or worse. Abuse can also be psychological. For example, threatening not to pay bills, threatening to harm or take children, or making a person live in constant fear. Abuse is not a light matter and it doesn't just go away. Don't cover it up and don't blame yourself. Get help. The toll-free number, Web site, and TTY of the National Domestic Violence Hotline are provided in the resource list at the back of the book.

9. Beware of the male ego monster.

The Tin Man has a very sensitive ego and it causes him to be extremely defensive. Remember Chapter Three, "How Men Translate What Women Say into Tin Speak? Translation into Tin Speak is what happens when the male ego monster rears its ugly head. When the Tin Man feels that he's vulnerable, his manhood is being questioned, his authority is being questioned, or he's being told what to do, he gets defensive (also see "How to Recognize Tin Speak," Chapter Two).

For example:

Wife/Girlfriend: Honey, I'm going to bed. Don't forget that it's your turn to do the dishes tonight. (She kisses Tin Man on the forehead.)

What Tin Man Hears: *I know you know it is your night to do the dishes. I'm just nagging you.*

Tin Man: I know that. I'm not going to forget. I'll do them when the game is over.

Wife/Girlfriend: Okay, well . . . could you at least fill up the sink with water during the next commercial? I'm afraid the rice will stick to the pots.

What Tin Man Hears: *I'm calling the shots around here. I asked you nicely the first time. Turn off that game, get off your butt, and go bust some suds right now!*

Tin Man (turning into the male ego monster and exploding like a volcano): I said I'll do them after the game!

This little scene won't have a happy ending. As you can see, it's all in the perception. She didn't make an unreasonable request, but he was so busy guarding his ego that he took it the wrong way.

10. Be a friend.

Don't assume a sterile and rigid role in his life under the name of wife or girlfriend. Continue to discover new ground in your relationship in all areas, especially your spiritual bonding. To grow and last, your marriage or relationship has to be about more than good sex, looking cute, spending holidays together, and going to the movies on Friday nights. Practice connecting from the inside. This is good for the Tin Man's reluctance to communicate. Just start by having some good conversations about things in which you both have an interest. Encourage him to open up as well as to listen.

11. Don't sleep on a time bomb.

Does the relationship hurt? Are you always wondering where he is and what he's doing? Do you fight more than you talk? Are you down in the doldrums most of the time, then up in the romantic clouds for a moment only to crash back down to the ground harder than the last time? Is your relationship at its best only when you're having sex? Are you seeing a married or otherwise committed man? Does your husband or boyfriend cheat? Are you cheating? Are you living in fear?

If you answered yes to any of those questions, you're probably sleeping on a time bomb.

There's no honor in living in a hellish relationship. You're not proving anything except that you can destroy yourself (and often your children as well). If you're finding that you're drawn, trapped, or addicted to a toxic relationship, there's something in you that needs to be healed. If you can't disconnect yourself, seek counseling so you can address your issues and gain the wholeness and self-confidence you need to free yourself. Or perhaps therapy for the two of you as a couple is the answer. But above all, if you're sleeping on a time bomb, the worst explosion is yet to come. Something has to change. If as a couple you're not actively working toward change, it's time to save yourself (and your kids, if you have children).

Reality Check #15: *A single and complete person is happier than a person who is spiritually and emotionally suffocating in a toxic relationship.*

Points to Remember

- Understand that our society encourages men to be Tin Men. But men must make their own choice as to whether they will unlearn that thinking.
- Teach your son to experience his full range of feelings.
- Make it safe for your husband/boyfriend, male relatives, and male friends to feel it's acceptable to share their feelings and emotions with you.
- Don't encourage men to be emotionally numb macho robots.
- View men as human beings with feelings.

Things to Think About

1. Do many women make the mistake of overnurturing grown men? Why or why not?

2. Why do some women try to change men?

3. As a girl, what behaviors did you grow up seeing as normal between men and women?

4. As a boy, what behaviors did you grow up seeing as normal between men and women?

TRY THIS
For Women
1. Write down the names of young boys and teenage boys with whom you have a personal relationship or for whom you have an influential role.

2. Next to each name make some notes about some situations you've encountered with them such as: times they've asked for your advice; situations in which you've had to correct their behavior; advice you've given them on key issues, such as sex, drugs, alcohol, venereal disease, domestic violence, etc.

3. What sort of things have they seen you do? What sort of things have they heard you say? Do you believe your relationship with these boys will positively or negatively affect their views of women?

TRY THIS
For Men
1. Write down the names of the women who were most significant in raising you.

2. Next to each name write notes about your memories of what each woman taught you about life.

3. Were any of those memories lessons about how to act as a man? In what way did each of those women influence the views you now have of manhood?

Chapter 14

"Honey, We Need to Talk"

Communicating with a Tin Man is difficult because Tin Men get defensive when their wives or girlfriends want to discuss relationship issues. Probably no other phrase known to humankind illicits more fear and panic in Tin Men than the words "Honey, we need to talk." Almost inevitably, we know these words will be followed by something that we won't like. It's never, "Honey, we need to talk. I like the way you cut the grass." Never is it "Honey, we need to talk. I just got you a new Corvette." Instead it's going to be something tough for us, something that will require us to tap our emotions or place ourselves in a vulnerable position.

Reality Check #16: *Communication is about sharing feelings and emotions, not fighting.*

Knowing Our Own Motives

Again, I'm speaking here from my experiences as a Tin Man. The first big block in communications for Tin Men comes from not knowing, or in some cases, not actually being aware of, our own motives. Before we get into serious conversations or arguments with our significant other, we should consider our own motives.

- Do we have a hidden agenda?
- Are we intending to dump our anger, frustrations, or rage on our significant other?

- Are we attempting to control our significant other?
- Are we arguing because we aren't saying what we really feel?

These are all different ways in which even well-intentioned communications will crumble down into arguments. In these situations, the Tin Man, and perhaps his significant other, haven't first taken the time to figure out where they're coming from. But that's often what an argument is, an explosion, not a moment of reasoning. But instead of lashing out, we should first look inside ourselves. Before we start a conversation about a sensitive issue, much less an argument, we should think about where we're coming from. Is it a place of love? Is our intention to improve the situation; or are we lashing out from anger, frustration, rage, or fear? What do we want to accomplish?

The Tin Man Needs to Listen

Our second big block in communications comes from listening. We may hear the other person's words, but are we listening? We have to listen in order to gain an understanding of what the other person is saying. Of course understanding what a person is saying doesn't mean we'll agree with her. But it will give a civility to the dialogue and guarantee that both people at least have the satisfaction of presenting their side. Sometimes that is enough in itself, because the other person just wanted to be heard. But even when we agree to disagree, it's better to do it from a well-informed perspective than to have given in to the temptation to shut off our minds because we don't agree. *It takes ongoing practice to listen patiently to someone we don't agree with, especially when we have strong feelings about an issue.*

The Tin Man's Barriers to Listening

1. Interrupting

When we interrupt someone who's trying to make a point in a disagreement, it's possible that at that moment we're being self-righteous by not listening to what the other person has to say. It's also possible that some people interrupt because they know they're wrong but don't want to face it. Interruptions keep us from getting all the information we need in order to gain an understanding. Interruptions also intensify arguments by making the person who's been cut off even more angry.

2. Raising the shield

The Tin Man will often raise the shield in disagreements. This is a defensive move done in anticipation of being attacked. John Gray described this line of male thinking in *Men Are from Mars, Women Are from Venus*. "When women want to talk about problems, men usually resist. A man assumes she is talking with him about her problems because she is holding him responsible. The more problems, the more he feels blamed. He does not realize that she is talking to feel better. A man doesn't know that she will appreciate it if he just listens."

3. Judging

This happens when the Tin Man listens, but instead of being objective, he acts as judge and jury of the person with whom he's in disagreement. The judging person is usually listening with a bias and will selectively hear only what serves to prove his own point. It often results in blaming or attempting playing the role of "know-it-all."

4. Selective hearing

Only hearing a little of what a person is saying and shutting out everything else she has to say is the Tin Man's style of selective hearing. This particularly happens in an argument when his hot buttons are hit. For example, when the Tin Man starts to feel threatened, he gets defensive and doesn't listen anymore. All he hears is Tin Speak (see Chapter Two). But the difference between this and interrupting is that in this situation he doesn't actually stop the other person. He simply allows her to continue to speak until it is his turn. But when she's finished, Tin Man didn't hear all of what she said, only the part he wanted to hear.

5. *Closed mind*

The closed mind is the number one enemy of communication. When the Tin Man closes his mind and refuses to even consider the point of the other person, he short-circuits the entire communication process. No meaningful discussion or communication can be achieved when one of the people won't even listen.

Couples Should Fight Fairly!

When communication fails, a couple's discussion deteriorates into an argument. That's when a couple gets on dangerous ground because Tin Men are notoriously insensitive in arguments. This is the time when a thoughtless word or action can cause a deep wound or even be the end of the relationship. But even an argument doesn't have to turn into a war if the Tin Man (and his significant other) agree to fight fairly.

When in an argument, always avoid:

INSIDE INSULTS
Personalized insults are the little inside bits of information that you have about a person that can trigger instant pain. These are usually things they have entrusted you with. Using this insider knowledge in an argument is hitting below the belt.

THE PAST

Don't bring up past experiences to belittle, shock, or slam someone. The past is almost never relevant.

TEASING

Teasing can make a person feel dishonored or ashamed and is never constructive to solving a disagreement.

INTIMIDATION

Avoid doing things that could escalate the argument to a physical level. These things could possibly be interpreted as physical threats:

- Blocking a person's path if he or she is trying to leave the room
- Pointing at a person while shouting
- Excessive shouting and swearing
- Following closely behind a person
- Standing over a person while shouting
- Shouting into someone's face
- Holding any object in a manner that looks threatening
- Throwing things around the room

NEVER *make any physical contact*!
Do not:

- Jab a person with your finger
- Squeeze his or her arm
- Throw anything at him or her
- Push him or her
- Slap or punch him or her
- Kick him or her

CREATE A SAFE ZONE

For years we've been telling kids to take a time-out. Perhaps we
need one, too. Agree on a neutralizing practice that you and your
significant other will use when tempers flare. This neutralizing
practice is your safe zone, and both must agree to honor it as a
way to cool down during an argument. My wife and I hold hands
and pray. It's actually a cooling act in itself, because in a disagreement it reminds us of the higher purpose of our relationship.
You can also try deep breathing, going to separate rooms, or
counting to one hundred by twos. Whatever method you use, having a safe zone is a good way to calm down. It will help both people find the peace necessary to disagree and engage in a meaningful
exchange of ideas instead of an argument.

Struggling for Power or Solutions?

Ideally, a couple would never disagree or argue about anything.
But that's impossible because couples are made of two individuals.
And two people will also have two sets of sometimes differing
opinions on things. But disagreements aren't bad; they're actually
a part of the growth of a relationship. That is, if they're conducted
in the right spirit.

A couple can go two ways in a disagreement: seek a solution
or struggle for power. *Seeking a solution requires both people to acknowledge that they would rather have peace than to fight.* Again, this
doesn't at all mean they agree 100 percent on everything all the
time. Nor does it mean they don't have heated disagreements.
What it does mean, however, is that even during a disagreement,
they're both interested in finding the solution, even when it is to
agree on disagreement. A couple that is seeking solutions together
and not struggling for power against each other will actually grow
from what they experience in a disagreement because they remain
love-based throughout the conflict.

On the other hand, the power struggle is a big issue that blocks effective communication for the Tin Man (and Tin Woman). When a man and a woman are gridlocked in a power struggle, they aren't actually attempting to communicate. Instead they're battling for control, and any and everything they disagree on or argue about is not so much about the topic of their discussion as it is about the issue of who's going to win.

Since a power struggle involves a winner and a loser, it always leaves a relationship out of balance; someone is bound to feel humiliated, hurt, or degraded. As a result of the loss felt from the argument, that person may counterstrike to regain some control or let anger simmer until the next argument. In essence, in a power struggle, things are never really at peace because one person is always attempting to dominate the other. *It doesn't matter whether the man or the woman is winning the power struggle; power struggles destroy the foundation of a relationship—trust and interdependence.*

Repair the Damage

Tin Men don't realize the importance of an apology. Arguments leave wounds that must be healed to bring a relationship back to full strength. The wounds caused by hurling angry words or harsh treatment must be repaired. Though it's not easy for the Tin Man to do, it's very necessary. Apologies are simple; only the two words "I apologize." But those two words are the gateway to healing.

Reality Check #17: *An apology is a powerful remedy.*

The other side to apologizing is forgiving. Forgiving someone is something we must do for ourselves. When we don't forgive we walk around with anger and resentment. Those feelings rage inside of us and hold us hostage to something in our past, which in turn prevents our enjoyment of the present. We have to let go of what happened and move on. Accepting an apology doesn't always heal the damage. Nor does it always mean that we will remain in a relationship after the fact. But it does create peace of mind for both people.

Reality Check #18: *Forgiveness gives you peace of mind.*

Things to Think About

1. If you're in a relationship, do your arguments with your significant other feel more like contests or solution-seeking discussions?

2. Have you been in any relationships that were power struggles? What role did you play in creating that situation?

3. Are you a good listener?

4. What has experience taught you about communication with the opposite sex?

TRY THIS
For Women
Consider the following four situations. How could you communicate the following ideas in a way that is both direct and tactful?
1. You want to communicate a desire for expression of more affection in your relationship.

2. You want to communicate an issue concerning income or paying bills.

3. You want to communicate an issue concerning your sex life together.

4. You want to communicate that a member of his family or close friend of his is getting on your nerves.

TRY THIS
For Men
Ask your significant other, a close female relative, or female friend, to share a concern or issue she is dealing with. As she shares with you, refrain from:
1. Feeling blamed or responsible (unless you really are).

2. Lecturing to her about what she did wrong.

3. Seeking to be the problem solver.

Just listen!
    After you've listened, if she wants your advice, offer tactful suggestions, remembering that you don't necessarily have to create the all-in-one solution to her problem.

Chapter 15

BUILDING THE BRIDGE TO INTIMACY, ONE STEP AT A TIME

I'll never forget the night I crossed the bridge to intimacy. It was a cool evening in late November when my wife and I were still dating. She'd invited me to come and watch her daughter dance in "The Nutcracker." The plan was to watch the show and then we'd all have dinner at her house afterward.

Although I agreed to go, I had a big problem with this date. Through the eyes of the Tin Man, this invitation was much more than just a date. As a Tin Man, I translated Jamey's invitation to a family event as an attempt by her to corral me into a more serious relationship, making a move in some sort of grand scheme to ultimately get married. I was especially sensitive to the timing of this invitation because it came when we had come to that critical point all dating couples reach, the time when you both know you either have to take things to another level or move on. In my Tin Man mind-set, going to that performance would be consenting to having a serious relationship. Not to mention that it was Christmas and most Tin Men start feeling really skittish around that time—too many expectations.

But despite all of my concerns, I went anyway. At the time, I didn't want to admit it, but the reason I went was because I knew this could be a turning point for me and that I could somehow break out of my tin armor and experience a close and loving connection with Jamey. That's what I was thinking deep inside. But on the surface, my mind was reeling from a loud inner dialogue.

It was a battle of two clear and opposing voices: the voice of Fear vs. the voice of Love.

Fear said, "Look, man. You're about to screw up. This babe is trying to get serious. Just pull off the freeway, turn around, and go back home. Tell her something came up. Then when she gives you static, you can tell her things are moving too fast and you need some space, or something. Come on, brother, it's Saturday night, we can hook up with the boys later and cruise the strip with the top down. We can call up some honeys who aren't trying to get serious and play some bedroom sports."

Love listened patiently as Fear presented his shaky case. Then Love said to me in a calming voice, "William, Fear doesn't have your best interests at heart. He's throwing distractions at you to try and cover up your real desire to connect in an intimate way. He knows that if you connect with the intimacy inside you, you'll become a new man; a man who embraces intimacy and faces his vulnerabilities. Fear doesn't want you to do that because that will leave him jobless. You know in your heart that you really want to feel a deep, soul-to-soul connection in this relationship. You want it and that's really what you're hoping to accomplish tonight, isn't it?"

I didn't have an answer for Love's question. I kept driving forward and Fear never stopped blabbing. By the time I reached the theater, I was at a critical turning point. At sometime or another, every Tin Man comes to this point—the point at which he has to make the decision whether or not to embrace intimacy. For me the turning point was deciding to walk into that theater, knowing that it was my acceptance of the fact that I was going to put my heart on the line. I knew I could still turn back and say good-bye to this situation. I could go back into the shell where I could continue to avoid intimacy, or I could remain open to the possibilities. With Fear walking with me, step for step, I took a deep breath and went through the doors of the theater.

I sat through "The Nutcracker" with my heart thumping and

palms sweating. I was distant toward Jamey, looking at her as little as possible and offering dry, short discussion when she tried to talk during intermission and after the show.

"Since you don't know your way around the neighborhood, you can follow me to my house from here," she said. She also gave me directions in case we got separated.

Unknown to her, I was starting to have a change of plans. During the show, the voice of Fear had gotten the best of me. I didn't want to have dinner. I wanted to leave. The courage I felt earlier had seeped away as I sat thinking about all the potential heartaches that come with the vulnerabilities of a relationship. What I needed was an excuse. "I need to get back." I leaned back on a pole to give me a casual look that I hoped would cover up how nervous I really was. "Aaa . . . I promised my mother I would swing by with some bananas she needs for a pudding she's making." I couldn't believe I said that.

"You look funny. Is something wrong?" she said with a skeptical look on her face.

"Nothing's wrong." I faked a laugh.

Jamey later told me that my eyes were big, and I looked like I'd seen a ghost; I had what she described as a "fear face." But there's an interesting side note as to why she could read the fear on my face: She'd experienced that "too frightened to go forward, yet knowing you shouldn't go back" feeling about me, too. Women grapple with intimacy just as men do, which is why she was wise enough not to pressure me. Instead, she said, "Well, if you feel like coming over, you're invited. But if not, I'll talk to you tomorrow."

And that's what brought me face to face with my fear of intimacy. Oddly enough, the option she gave me wasn't the answer the Tin Man in me wanted to hear. I was actually hoping she would try to pressure me. Then I could put her into the desperate and emotionally clingy category and I would feel justified about putting an end to the relationship. But since she didn't pressure me and give me the easy excuse, I now had to face the facts about my avoidance of intimacy. Now the ball was in my court. The question was clear: *Why are you still standing here, William July?*

It was that realization that made me go left when I was supposed to go right as I followed Jamey out of the parking lot. Again, fear of intimacy gripped me. I decided I couldn't do it. I didn't want to take the chance of putting my heart on the line. Fear laughed. Love shook its head. In my gut, I didn't feel right. Jamey was a woman I truly loved from the inside out. I felt a closeness to her, not only romantically but in a pure and spiritual way. So why was I running? And what was I running *to*? Those are the questions Love asked me. Questions I couldn't answer.

I turned around and headed back in the right direction. By this time, I had lost sight of her. I know she knew why I turned left. But I still tried to cover my tracks. I stopped at a grocery store and bought some bananas. When I got to her house, I smiled when she answered the door. "I had to stop for the bananas," I said. She just laughed. Over dinner, I told her what I was going through. And she reassured me that she understood because she'd had her own moments of fear.

Several days later, my attitude toward intimacy had changed and my tin armor had fallen away because I'd found my heart. On Christmas Eve, I went to church with Jamey and her daughter. This time my hands weren't sweaty and my heart wasn't pounding. I didn't fight the closeness I felt because sharing my love felt so good; it felt peaceful and right. That is a comfort that I'd never have found living in fear of intimacy.

Two Four-Letter Words: Fear and Love

The Tin Man's avoidance of intimacy is really about fear. He's afraid his feelings will make him vulnerable and leave him open to getting hurt. He's afraid that expressing his feelings may not look masculine. Or he could be afraid because he's never gotten to know his feelings enough to trust them.

Fear causes us to distrust our better judgment, the little voice we all hear that tells us what's right. Instead, fear causes us to react to things in an irrational way. For example, fear causes us to take jobs we hate (or remain in), and causes us to get into relationships for the wrong reasons (or to stay in bad relationships that are not working). When issues arise that require the Tin Man to use his feelings, it's fear that causes him to close himself off from them or lash out in an aggressive way.

Overcoming fear of his feelings is a tall order for the Tin Man. To do this he needs to replace the fear that imprisons him with the motivating power of love. I'm not referring to romance, I'm speaking of a higher love that empowers us to live by faith. The Tin Man lives to gratify his lust for power, money, and sex. But to transform himself, he has to realize that those things are not really capable of satisfying him. Actually, the pursuit of power, money, and sex leaves him empty because the more he gets, the more he needs.

When the Tin Man finally realizes he can't ever be satisfied strictly by accumulating things or by physical gratification, he'll turn to his inner vision and start seeking a connection with God. That's when he will learn to live by love, trusting and relying on his inner vision. And that is what transforms his weakened life into a powerful one. *Love is not only the foundation of thriving personal relationships; it also promotes a peace of mind and success in every other area of life as well.*

Letting go of fear and living by love is the way the Tin Man can build his bridge to intimacy. It's ultimately the only way to thrive. We actually don't have any choice but to live by love, although it isn't always apparent to us. We sometimes don't realize that love is the way until we've been knocked down from our pedestals of ego, pride, and power.

Ten Ways for Tin Men to
Start Focusing on More Intimacy

First, I have to be honest and say this isn't an overnight process. I would love to say it's as simple as going to the store and buying some sort of gadget to put under your head while you sleep, but that's just not true. Developing intimacy in your life is a spiritual healing process, a transformation, and it takes time—so be patient. Think of a Tin Man who is changing his life as a work in progress. He's a potential masterpiece that could take months or years to complete.

There can be no easy and foolproof formula for the Tin Man to connect to intimacy, because each man must confront the issues unique to his situation. But for those who are serious about making a change for the better, the following suggestions can help make the transition from Tin Man to complete man a little easier:

1. Don't lie to yourself about wanting to change.

One of my Tin Man friends used to call me and say, "Man, I'm going to be good from now on"—meaning he was going to give up his playboy lifestyle. But he was always laughing when he said those words because he knew he wasn't serious. He was just having a fleeting moment of guilt, probably from all the lies he'd been telling women. It's simple: A man who doesn't possess a sincere desire to change isn't going to be successful at becoming more intimate and sensitive. If you're not ready for a serious intimate relationship, if you're not ready to change, don't fool yourself. And most important, don't pretend you're ready when you know you're not.

2. Stop being a flirt.

There was a time when flirting was like a sport to me. But when I recovered from being a Tin Man, I stopped flirting. I'm referring to gratuitous flirting as conversation or gestures that go beyond the lines of good taste (you fellas know what I mean). As I looked at this issue in my life I realized that when you get down to it, flirting has one of two basic motives: It's either being done as an ego boost for the man who's flirting, or it's an attempt to create a sexual opportunity. Neither is productive behavior for a man trying to develop a meaningful and intimate relationship with a specific woman.

3. Go back to basics.

Single guys, take some of the dazzle out of your approach to women, be less "Mack Daddy" and more authentic. Develop a friendship first. In other words, don't try to impress women with your car, clothes, career, or meaningless conversation.

4. Catch yourself drifting.

When you see an attractive woman and your eyes beam like a magnet to her cleavage or behind, pull yourself back to sanity. There's nothing wrong with acknowledging that she looks great. But don't drift into fantasies or thoughts about what she looks like naked or what she'd be like in bed. Those thoughts cause you to look at women as sexual objects instead of people with whom you have intimate relationships.

5. Develop a lot of willpower.

You can't buy willpower, you have to develop it—and a recovering Tin Man needs lots of it. Just because you decide you're going to change doesn't mean everyone in the world will automatically change, too. You won't suddenly stop meeting women who flirt with and/or make sexual advances toward you. You'll still know the same guys that you used to frequent pickup bars and strip clubs with. And your buddies will still want to tell you stories of their sexual conquests. Resist the urge to indulge with them and you'll strengthen your willpower. You build willpower the same way you build muscle—by lifting weights and lots of repetition.

6. Hold hands and hug, just because.

When performed between two caring individuals, lovemaking is a sacred, intimate act. But intimacy doesn't have to be just sexual. If you're in a relationship, take some time to hold hands more. Start giving your wife or girlfriend a hug for no reason other than to hold her. Most women like to cuddle, so try it every once in a while. You'll be surprised by the results.

7. Learn to put your words into feelings.

Here are three ways to say what you feel:

a. Just say it!

Sometimes you can think about something you want to say too long and eventually you'll talk yourself out of doing it. Or you rehearse it and it still doesn't come out the right way. Don't rehearse or think about what you have to say for too long. Don't get stuck into thinking about what might happen if you say what you feel; just say it. Use the same grab-the-bull-by-the-horns approach you use in business or sports.

b. Write a letter.

Write your feelings down in a letter and give it to your wife or girlfriend. This method is not as difficult for the Tin Man because it's one-way communication. And though it isn't a verbal exchange, it's better than not sharing your feelings. But you should still have a long-term goal of being able to say what you're feeling. Letters can get the point across, but they aren't always as effective as two-way dialogue.

c. Look at something else.

Some women probably won't like this. But it sure helps guys who are learning to communicate their feelings if someone isn't staring at them. Position yourself so that you don't have to look directly at her while you talk. Just about any angle will work as long as your back isn't to her. For example, you could both face a window while you talk. It may sound like chickening out, but it's not. It's better than not talking about how you feel.

Note: If you use this technique, you should at least make eye contact every once in a while. It helps to reassure your significant other/spouse of your sincerity. Or if you find that you're not as uncomfortable as you thought you'd be, you may decide to sit face to face.

8. *Learn to say "I love you."*

Sounds simple, but far too many men have a rough time with this one. But when you can say this and mean it, you have overcome many of the fears that once kept you from experiencing your feelings. Again, there's no scientific method for doing this. But one of three previously discussed techniques (just saying it, writing a letter, or looking at something else) may help.

9. *Learn to show "I love you."*

Flowers and candy are nice. But women often say, "It's the little things that count most." Small gestures are a great way to express love. For example, my wife and I have agreed upon certain duties around the house. But sometimes, to show my love, I'll surprise her and do something that is her job (and she does the same for me). For example, if it's her turn to clean the kitchen, sometimes I'll do it. If it's her turn to cook, sometimes I'll do it.

10. *Show gratitude and respect for others.*

Some Tin Men have difficulty expressing gratitude and respect for other people. They find it difficult to say "thank you" or "please." Somehow they seem to feel that such words indicate weakness. But those words don't indicate weakness. Those words show other people that you appreciate and respect them. Appreciation and respect are some of the basic building blocks for any type of relationship.

What Does Doing All This Stuff Do for a Guy?

The rewards of shedding the tin armor are strong relationships, personal peace, and even a more fulfilling and profitable career. For me, shedding my tin armor created a completely new life. My changes were big. I stopped working just to make money and switched careers. I finally started doing what I love: writing and speaking. I stopped sleeping around and made a soul-to-soul connection with a woman and married her. I realized that health maintenance wasn't only about going to the gym but also about what I ate and how I managed stress. I also gained the good sense to visit a doctor regularly instead of waiting until I was so sick I had to drag myself into his office. And I alleviated a lot of stress from my life when I started living by faith. That allowed me to stop worrying about the future and to start enjoying the present.

Having said all that, I don't want to leave anyone with the impression that once a man sheds his armor he never feels the urge to slip back into some of his old ways. That's not the case. Resisting the urge to be a Tin Man involves constant upkeep.

Things to Think About

1. Have you had an experience in which you confronted your avoidance of intimacy? Did you embrace intimacy or run from it? Why?

2. What are your greatest fears about being intimate with another person? How can you overcome them?

3. Which of the ten ways to start focusing on intimacy are easy for you? Which are most difficult? Why?

TRY THIS
For Women and Men

Create the Life You Want
1. Write a list of affirmations for yourself, a list of your goals and dreams. Focus mainly on larger concepts, not only on career and material goals. It's important to speak in the affirmative and in the present tense. Avoid indefinite terms such as "One day I'll . . ."; "My dream is to . . ."; "I think I will . . ." Use wording that creates the life you want right now. Put the wheels of progress in motion now by saying it and believing it; then your words will become reality. For example: "I love and respect myself," "I'm only in relationships that enhance my life," "I am financially successful," "I honor my family," "I am successfully finishing school," "I have a wonderful home," etc.

Read your affirmations or say them aloud before going to bed at night and first thing when you rise in the morning. You should also revise your affirmations from time to time, keeping them current with the circumstances in your life. You can also make a recording of your voice reciting your affirmations over your favorite instrumental music.

2. Daydream. Put on some of your favorite music and imagine yourself achieving your goals. Picture specific goals and situations. Don't limit yourself as to what those things are. Include details. How are you dressed? What time of day is it? Where are you? Who is with you?

3. Create a visualization book. A visualization book takes affirmations a step farther by associating them with an actual image.

To create a visualization book do the following:

a. Write or type all of your affirmations on plain white paper. Leave enough space between each line to cut with scissors.

b. Cut out each affirmation and trim away the excess paper.

c. Find magazines, newspapers, or artwork that express the ideas that you have on your affirmation list. While doing this, you may also run across actual words or phrases that match your affirmations. Cut them out, too. For example, if you want to travel, cut out a picture of an airplane and several places you want to visit. At the bottom of the page, paste the affirmation "I travel." My travel affirmation page has pictures of the great pyramids of Egypt, beaches, and mountains.

d. Glue the affirmations and the images you've cut onto white pages. What I do is glue my affirmations and images onto removable pages in a photo album. This allows me to turn the pages of my visualization book easily as I go through it.

Note: Your list of affirmations and your visualization book are highly confidential. Don't feel compelled to share them with anyone unless you are absolutely sure the person will respect the contents. Don't allow anyone to spoil your positive energy with his or her negativity.

Chapter 16

Twenty-eight Ways to Change Your Life Right Now

Here's a list of twenty-eight more things the Tin Man can do to break out of his tin armor. Applying these things to your life will help you create a more intimate relationship with yourself and the world around you.

1. Have a heart.

Cherish your spouse/significant other and your family. Don't take their love for granted. Open your heart and let them in. Don't let your only interaction with them be mindless routine. Plan to spend quality time with them, laugh with them, play with them. And extend this love beyond your family. Have a heart when dealing with friends, coworkers, and even the people you pass on the sidewalk every day. Be kind, friendly, and courteous. Be less defensive and develop a pleasant demeanor. Don't get me wrong: I'm not suggesting that you become a wimp, but there's a great deal of strength in being open and kind.

2. Be honest.

Remember the old adage "Honesty is the best policy"? Cliché, yes, but true nonetheless. I believe that honesty is the anchor of intimacy. But to engage in an intimate relationship with another person you have to be honest with yourself first. Does intimacy scare you? Is it something you want to experience but don't feel you can? Have you thought about it and truly aren't ready for an intimate connection? The next step is to be honest about intimacy in your personal relationships. You don't need to tell every woman you meet that you're working through some intimacy issues. But when you decide to get serious with a particular woman, commit to establishing intimacy in your relationship—speak from the heart and talk honestly about your feelings. Speak honestly about intimacy so it doesn't become a monster lurking around waiting to strike down your relationship.

3. Learn to commit.

Tin Men are accustomed to living disconnected lives. They try to get the benefits of a relationship without making a commitment. But in doing so, they not only shortchange their significant other but themselves, too. To experience the full power and beauty of a fulfilling relationship, Tin Men have to shed their defenses, be themselves, and fully commit themselves to making the union work.

4. Trust your feelings.

Don't put all your trust in facts and figures and overlook your intuition. That gut feeling you get about things is God's voice telling you what is right for your life. Part of breaking out of the tin armor is learning to see with more inner vision. Trust your feelings, not your defense mechanisms. Let your instincts guide you.

5. Communicate, communicate, communicate.

One of the biggest challenges in any relationship is communication. Say what's on your mind when dealing with others, but do it thoughtfully, with tact. Holding your feelings in will only make you tense, angry, or sad. The other major part of good communication is learning to listen. Don't interrupt, be open-minded, and wait until you've heard all the facts before responding.

6. Start asking for help.

Interdependence is the key to life. The idea that we can do something completely on our own is an illusion. Nobody has ever done anything totally on his own and nobody ever will. Create support systems in your personal life, network with others in your profession. Human beings are designed to create great things together.

7. Don't hang on to a dead-end relationship.

Most people who are in a dead-end relationship are well aware of it but don't want to admit it. Are you in denial about your dead-end relationship? Do you see the brick wall approaching but hope something will magically change a situation that has been getting progressively worse? Don't cling to a situation that you know isn't working. But first, check yourself. Have you done all you can do? If you have, try to resolve the situation amicably. Pursuing a relationship that isn't working is a disservice to you and the other person.

8. Don't hurry into a new relationship.

Being in a good relationship is a wonderful experience, but it's not the only way to enjoy life. When we're not in a relationship, we can take time to improve our relationship with ourselves. Instead of feeling like something is missing from your life, realize that being single is a great time for personal growth. The time you spend developing yourself for your own enrichment and gratification will change your life and will also benefit the person who will enter your life later.

9. Develop relationships based on intimacy, not sex.

Sex alone does not create a close and fulfilling relationship between two people, not even committed or married couples. Get to know your significant other/spouse from the inside out instead of the outside in. Talk, exchange secrets, develop a close emotional bond. Sex combined with intimacy is sacred to a couple. But without intimacy, sex is only a physical act. It may be gratifying to the body but not the soul.

10. Wherever you go, there you are.

Sometimes people think moving to a new place will solve all of their problems; and sometimes it does help to move to another neighborhood, state, or even another country. But the act of moving is not what creates a new direction. You can't run from problems and issues. If you board a plane in Atlanta to escape a problem, it will be waiting for you when you land in Chicago. The most important move you can make is to change your mind-set. So before you make an external move that you think will change your life, remember: "Wherever you go, there you are."

11. Don't allow work to rule your life.

Free time is precious. Often the only way to have more free time is to work faster. But if we're not careful, that leisure time we're working so hard to create doesn't materialize. Sometimes we get so caught up working to get ahead of schedule that we replace leisure time with more work. As a result, we get farther "ahead," but we're actually more stressed out. If you feel your work schedule is out of control, do something about it. Plan a vacation, take a day off, or commit to leaving the office at a certain time no matter what.

12. Don't overextend yourself.

Every day has twenty-four hours, so you only have a certain amount of time and energy at your disposal. You don't have enough energy to be superworker at the job, superparent at home, superchild to your parents, and supercitizen to the PTA, homeowner's association, every political campaign, or church activity that pops up. And let's not forget superlover to your spouse or significant other. Since you can't do everything, prioritize your time and use it wisely.

13. Develop friendships.

Friendships with people who sincerely love and care for you are worth their weight in gold. These are the people who will be happy with you in the good times and will give you a reassuring hug when you're low. It's important to cultivate these relationships with love through action. Pause to call your friends regularly. Spend time with them. Support them in their goals and endeavors.

14. Learn to appreciate what you have.

In the book of Philippians, 4:11, the apostle Paul writes ". . . I have learned to be content whatever the circumstances." That wisdom reminds us that we should check our motives when it comes to the constant striving to get more. How much is enough? Why are we always trying to get more? Ask yourself what you're really seeking. Underneath much of the voracious consumption and drive for more money and power we'll often find more basic desires that are unmet—the desire to share love with another person, to have real friends, to feel secure, or to have peace of mind. Those things can't be achieved by more money, sex, power, drugs, alcohol, etc. Instead of always reaching for more, first realize and appreciate what you already have.

15. Learn to let go of negative feelings.

When tension, anger, anxiety, or fear grip the Tin Man, he loses his cool. He makes bad decisions and lashes out at those around him. The more he tries to control his surroundings, the more the stress of holding it all together consumes him. Several times throughout the day, stop for a moment. Simply close your eyes and take a few deep breaths. Relax your shoulders, hands, and face. Believe it or not, the more you let things go, the calmer you'll become. This helps you to become steady so you'll make the right decisions and do what's best for yourself and all others concerned.

16. Get some rest.

It's impossible to function at your best if you don't get any rest. Get the amount of sleep that your body requires to feel your best. When possible, use a vacation or personal day and take off from work. And remember, don't fill holidays and vacations with so much travel and so many activities that you don't get any rest during your time off.

17. Exercise regularly.

Clear your mind and rejuvenate the body with regular exercise. You don't need to join an expensive health club or start a complicated exercise routine. Just engage in moderate exercise (for example, walking) for twenty to thirty minutes every other day. If you do go to the gym to work out, remember that you don't have to be Hercules. Moderation and consistency are the keys to a successful exercise plan.

18. Simplify your life.

Rid your life of confusion. What's stressing you? Check your schedule, your job, your home, and your personal relationships for unnecessary stress. Then take steps to make your life more simple. A simpler life is a more peaceful life.

19. Maintain a positive attitude.

Attitude is everything. Your attitude determines your perception of the world around you. When you have a positive outlook on life, you'll discover wonderful opportunities and happiness because you expect to. But the minute you feel that life is terrible and there's no hope, your life will become flooded with negativity and you won't be able to recognize a good opportunity. A positive attitude doesn't make life a yellow brick road, but it does keep us from becoming our own worse enemy.

20. *Avoid compromising situations.*

We all know what things we should or shouldn't do to create peace, health, and real happiness in our lives. It would be easy to do the right thing if we didn't ever feel temptation. But at some point in your life, you'll be tempted to do something you shouldn't do. In your effort to avoid temptation, you may find it necessary to make new friends, people who will encourage you to live a healthier lifestyle. By all means do that, but don't just toss your old friends in the trash; let them know you're not the person you used to be. Then, if they want you to do the things you used to do with them, stick to your principles. But please note, if you're having a problem with an addiction, contact a counselor specializing in the area in which you need help.

21. *Smile more.*

It takes many more muscles to smile than it takes to frown. Smiles are gateways to positive experiences. By smiling you share positive energy that others can either return to you or pass along to someone else. A frown or scowl shuts you off from other people and may prevent you from having a positive experience. As Patti LaBelle says, "Don't block the blessings." Think about it: When was the last time you tried to hold a conversation with a person who was frowning at you?

22. *Learn to let go (and let God).*

Are you a supercaretaker or control freak? The supercaretaker attempts to be the sole and absolute source of someone else's every need: financial, emotional, and physical. Give yourself a break and learn to connect with others and find ways to share tasks and responsibilities. If you're a control freak and feel that you must have absolute power and control over a person or situation to determine the outcome, here's an important newsflash: Learn to let go and let God. You might as well relax, because you'll never have total control over anything or anyone but yourself!

23. Be flexible.

Instead of attempting to make things and people behave exactly the way you want, be flexible. It is not within our capacity as human beings to conquer and control everything. It may seem that way sometimes. We may have that illusion, Tin Men in particular. But it doesn't take long for reality to topple even the biggest conqueror. On the contrary, when we become flexible and able to change with changing circumstances we get much better results.

24. Eat better.

Food fuels the body the way gasoline fuels cars. When cars have high-quality fuel, they run better. When you fuel your body with good food, it will run better, too. When we don't consume the nutrients that give our bodies the necessary fuel to thrive, we don't reach our full optimum potential. Improper nutrition slows us down, robs us of energy, and can even make us ill. A commitment to eating better doesn't necessarily mean that we can never have another cheeseburger. But we do need to reshape our attitudes about food. We need to see food as fuel for our cells and not something that will provide stress relief if we overindulge.

25. Change jobs or start a new career.

We change jobs and careers for many reasons. Sometimes we outgrow our occupations. Sometimes we grow tired of the office politics, or we feel our potential isn't being utilized in the right way. Maybe we've been passed over for promotion too many times. Life is too short to spend an excessive amount of time working in a place that you hate or in a career you don't love. When faced with a job or career change, don't view it as throwing away your years of experience and training. Instead see it as part of your continuing growth as a person, each experience building on the previous. There may be opportunities to transfer within your company. There could be another company or firm looking for a person with your experience and skills. Maybe it's time for you to start your own business. Assess yourself, make a list of your skills, and investigate your options.

26. *Do what you love.*

Hard work can produce money but not necessarily fulfillment. The money earned through hard work alone can't compare to the money and fulfillment that come from doing what you love. When you're doing what you love you'll be successful because you won't see it as purely work, but as outright fun, something you love doing. Loving your work will allow your talents to take you to heights you never envisioned. This doesn't mean you'll be rich overnight, but you will eventually become more healthy, wealthy, and whole than you would doing something that you didn't love.

27. *Manage your money or it will manage you.*

Financial matters are a major source of stress in the lives of many people. But in lots of cases, much of the stress comes from mismanagement of the money we have, or from living beyond our means. I once heard a financial expert say that anybody could outspend their income. In other words, it doesn't matter if you earn twenty thousand or two hundred thousand dollars per year; you can easily spend more than you make. It's all relative. Without a budget and some self-discipline we easily find ourselves swimming in debt and working overtime, if not two jobs. Though it is a reality that many people have to work very hard just to make ends meet, lots of us could make ends meet better if we

lived within our means. Scale back your lifestyle, stick to a budget, and save more.

28. Go back to school, get more training.

No matter what level of education you have or what you're
doing now, you could benefit from additional training and knowledge. When we allow ourselves to stop learning, we grow stag-
nant. If you want a college degree, or an advanced degree, attend
a university or graduate school on a part-time basis with a course
load that is comfortable for your schedule. Or sign up for training that is relevant to your career. Earn professional certifications
that lead to greater credibility and income. And don't forget the
third option: Just take some adult education classes that interest
you for the pure enjoyment of learning something new.

Things to Think About

1. Which item from the list had the most significance for you?
Why?

2. What things could you add to this list?

3. Is there anything on this list that you've already changed
about yourself?

TRY THIS
For Women and Men
Go through the twenty-eight things mentioned in this chapter and apply them to your life. As you read them, consider
what you might do to change your life.

- Which change would have an immediate positive effect on your life?
- Which change would be difficult in the beginning but beneficial in the long run?
- How will you activate positive changes in your life?

Though he should conquer a thousand men in the battlefield
a thousand times, yet he, indeed, who would conquer himself is
the noblest victor.
—*The Buddha*

Special Message 1

TO THE WOMEN WHO LOVE US: A CONVERSATION ABOUT MEN AND INTIMACY

Perhaps at times you find yourself frustrated, confused, or disillusioned with men. You've been through the same games over and over with so many different men. You've been understanding. You've tried to use supposedly time-tested "rules." And you've even thrown caution to the wind and gone with your feelings. But nothing has worked. The men you've been involved with continue to avoid genuine intimacy with you.

In this book, I haven't claimed to have a list of simple answers that will tell you why all men do what they do when it comes to intimacy. That's not possible or realistic and nobody should make such a claim. However, what I have done in this book is to bring out some important issues about men and intimacy. I've shown the important fact that men weren't born avoiding intimacy. That's something we've learned. I say this not as an excuse but as a reality. We were taught and accepted that we were to go out and conquer all before us and then to maintain control over our kingdoms. We bought into the idea that we had to carry the world on our backs. Into that category fell our jobs, women, children, etc. Who told us all this? Society.

And you as women were sold those ideas, too. Many of you were told your life would begin when you fell in love with a man, not with yourself. That your life would be defined by whom you married and your children. You were told to hold out for a Prince

Charming and fed delusions about the "good old days" being better than they actually were. Many of you were misinformed just
as we Tin Men were. We've all been misinformed and hurt by
these delusions, but you women have been affected most of all.

The question is what do we do now? What do men and women
who want better relationships do? Now we're facing each other,
both of us holding shattered dreams in our hands. How do we re-
build together? The answer is to drop our baggage. We're still
trying to live in roles that are hundreds of years old in a world that
has drastically changed. We use e-mail today, not smoke signals.
We travel by car, not by horse. When we're hungry, we don't go
out and kill buffalo and build a fire, we go to the supermarket and
fire up the gas grill. But ironically, our ideas about relationships
are still very antiquated. It's time for an update for both sexes.
Men can be masculine but sensitive, too. Women can be feminine
and strong. We can have rich relationships without one person
dominating the other.

Some suggestions for the women who love us:

- Realize there is no simple all-in-one solution for male-
  female relationships.
- Don't believe stereotypes or "rules" that cause you to
  make blanket assumptions about all men.
- Despite what you may have experienced or heard about
  the experiences of other women, keep an open mind
  about the man you're dating or involved with.
- Love doesn't require you to lose your dignity. Honor
  and respect yourself in all your relationships.

Special Message 2

To Single Mothers

"I wish I had a husband." These words were spoken in honest frustration by a single mother after she rattled off a list of all the things she had to do that evening before putting her kids to bed. It was a mind-boggling list of things. The moment she arrived home from her job downtown, she was feeding kids, washing clothes, running errands, and playing the role of homework tutor, not to mention paying bills and taking care of her daughter's cough. And she did this all-in-one parent routine day after day.

Understandably, her desire for a husband was a loaded wish. After listening to her schedule, I wondered what she meant. Did she mean "I wish I had some emotional support"? Did she mean "I wish I had some help paying these bills"? Did she mean "I wish I had some excitement and relief from my everyday routine"? Did she mean "I wish I had a good father figure for my kids"? At different times, I suppose it could mean one or all of those things. That desire for companionship and help is a legitimate feeling, but not always one that will come in the form of a husband. Believing that myth can lead a single mother into sadness, even despair. The kind of despair that leaves her vulnerable to the types of Tin Men who prey on women who feel they need a man to survive.

An option is to turn the issue around. Instead of wishing for a husband, she could focus on creating the things she wants in her life to ease her burdens and make life more complete for her children. There's absolutely nothing wrong with her wanting a husband. But there is life without one. And that can still be a good life for her and her kids. While an emotionally accessible, complete man in the house would be a great balance, it doesn't mean the lack of a man in the house means that she and the kids must feel incomplete. Single mothers, you may be the only parent in the lives of your children, but you can still open the world to them. You can be a great single parent by showing them a model of the kind of *person* they should aspire to be. It doesn't have to do with the money you make, degrees you have, or anything you own, for that matter. It has to do with the character you demonstrate. Life must go on without a man in the house.

Here are some other suggestions for single mothers:

- Never make a man more important than your children.
- Be conscientious about your dating habits around your children. They are learning about relationships from you.
- Don't introduce too many men to your children. They may get attached or become confused.
- Don't play and pet with different partners in front of your children.
- Claim the child support that rightfully belongs to you and your children.
- Don't allow them to feel that they're baggage left over from a bad relationship.
- Know that you're doing your best and feel good about it.
- Create a support system of relatives, friends, and professionals (therapist, religious facilitator, lawyer, mechanic, pediatrician, etc.).

Special Message 3

To African American Men

There are some specific challenges faced by African American men when it comes to the issue of manhood. Speaking frankly, achieving the American ideal of manhood has been an illusive goal for us. In American society, manhood has traditionally been defined by the ability to provide and protect. But historically, African American men were denied the ability to provide and protect. Even when the laws that blocked the progress of African Americans were removed, we found ourselves far behind in the economic and educational race and still facing a number of invisible, but real, economic, political, and social barriers.

However, because we are American men, we, too, find our definition of manhood to be built around the ideas of power, sex, and money. Ideas that double in frustration, rage, and pain for a group of men whose history has made it more difficult to achieve that definition of manhood in large numbers. So what do we do as African American men? Where is the new definition of manhood for us?

Redefining manhood for African American men begins with a re-creation of our image in our own minds, making a conscious separation from negative stereotypes of African American men. We have all experienced racism and discrimination. We've heard the racial slurs, jokes, and ignorant beliefs about us. These things can work in concert to ruin our self-esteem if we allow them to. To combat this, we must re-create our self-image through the realization that we are great men from a legacy of great men. The greatness of African American men is the reality of history but often overlooked. Read and study for yourself and you'll see that your heritage is rich with wise and powerful heroes.

But most important, the redefinition of manhood for African American or any men lies in our connection with God. For ultimately it is not another human being, laws, or economics that sustain or empower us. The ultimate well of power is found when our spirits are connected to the power that drives the universe. Connection with this power is a divine birthright of every human being. As human beings we have certain inalienable rights granted by God that no man has the right to take away. To that end, we are worthy and entitled to full participation in any- and everything in this world. We are not to live down to stereotypes but up to our full potential.

Some ideas for African American men:

- Foster fellowship with other African American men.
- Find some role models that look like you.
- Travel; it will build your appreciation for your culture and show you the oneness of the human race.
- Honor your heritage, but also respect the heritage of others.

Special Message 4

TO THE MEN OF THE OLD SCHOOL

You've come to a time when you can't judge yourself by your job because you've either retired or have had to slow your pace. You've come to a time when some of your friends and loved ones have started passing on. You've come to a time at which your sexual prowess can't be your definition of manhood because the effects of aging have taken their toll on your sexual vigor. And though drugs such as Viagra may help your sexual ability, that only addresses a physical situation, a mere Band-Aid over the true issues brought on by being a Tin Man in the golden years.

Aging and retirement are frightening prospects for Tin Men. This is because aging and retirement bring to the forefront the very issues Tin Men have been in denial about all their lives. Aging brings us to the reckoning that we aren't physically invulnerable and eternally virile. And retirement brings forth the fact that we have to have more meaning to our lives than our work. This can be a time of crisis for Tin Men. Particularly white males. Again I quote Royda Crose, Ph.D., author of *Why Women Live Longer Than Men*: "White men over sixty-five years of age present the highest suicide risk in our society. They have had more power, money, and privilege than women and ethnic minorities throughout life, yet they seem to be least prepared to cope with the issues of growing old."

But it's not just the white males. Tin Men of all sorts of backgrounds may find themselves feeling useless and even desperate in their later years because their very idea of what makes them a man has slipped away from them. Aging and retirement is a period in life during which Tin Men must seek to radically redefine themselves. But can a man who was born and raised by the old, hard-nosed conquer-and-control school of manhood change his mind-set and re-create himself in his golden years?

Yes, he can. Aging and retirement isn't an end, it's a beginning. A chance to start a new life and to experience many of the things and feelings you may have ignored during your life as a Tin Man. Here are some ideas to help you create your new beginning.

- If you have children, have a heart-to-heart talk with each of your children.
- Reminisce about some of your feelings from your childhood.
- Vent some of the frustrations you had in your career.
- If your wife is living, have a heart-to-heart talk with her.
- Visit a therapist to heal some old wounds that still plague you and put them to rest.
- Make plans to do something you've always wanted to do.
- Begin taking classes that interest you.
- Start walking or a light exercise program.
- Travel.
- Contact some friends you haven't spoken to in years.
- Create new friendships and emotional support systems.
- Ask for help when you know you need it!

Special Message 5

To the Young Guys

Avoiding the Tin Man mind-set in your late teens and early twenties requires lots of focus. This is because everyone around you is always filling your head with notions about how these are the best years of your life and you should just focus on having a good time. But their definition of a good time is often seeking sex simply for the sport of it or it involves getting drunk or high. As a young man, you'll find yourself bombarded with images and opinions of how you should act as a young single guy or eligible bachelor. Your challenge is to avoid at an early age buying wholesale into a self-destructive definition of manhood without first finding out where you actually feel comfortable in it all.

How do you survive this period in your life without succumbing to the overindulgences that lead to emotional numbness or get you off track with your spiritual center? The answer isn't to curl up behind a rock. *This is not the prescription for being a social outcast, geek, or introvert.* That's not living in the real world. But what you've got to do is draw the line between enjoyment of life and overindulgence. Enjoying the company of women and going to parties or clubs are not bad things. It's the indulgence in such things that causes you to lose focus. Indulgence leads you to seek your very meaning for life in the number of women you can sleep with, getting drunk, or feeling that you can't have fun unless you're at a party surrounded by other people. That's being out of balance. When your life is out of balance you're susceptible to seeking fulfillment through quick and easy temporary pleasures. But when you're well balanced, you don't need to overindulge in those things. You're at peace and able to keep your life in reasonable bounds that ultimately make you stronger in mind, body, and soul.

You don't have to be a social hermit. It doesn't mean you're not going to date different women. It doesn't mean you can't hang out with your friends or fraternity brothers. It doesn't necessarily mean you'll never have a drink. That's your decision, but if you do you'll be wise enough not to get drunk. At your age, you should know the difference between real fun and self-destructive behavior. Many young guys have already grown tired of trying to fit the traditional womanizing and partying idea of being a young bachelor. You may be one of them. Being different may make you feel odd, but you're not alone. Trust your intuition about what is right; it won't lead you wrong.

Some suggestions for the young guys:

- Surround yourself with friends who will encourage you to be alcohol- and drug-free. Spend time with guys who know how to have fun without engaging in violent, risky, or dangerous activities.
- Learn to recognize the difference between feeling lust and being in love.
- Don't enter into competition with other guys for the attention of women. Honor yourself.
- Realize that drugs and heavy drinking are not measures of manhood. They are self-destructive behaviors.
- Understand that women are human beings, not playtoys for your pleasure.
- Understand that children are human beings, not marks on a score card.
- Realize that kindness and sensitivity are not weaknesses.

THE MOST COMMONLY ASKED
QUESTIONS ABOUT TIN MEN

1. I have a problem communicating with my Tin Man. Why does he seem to misunderstand everything I say?
Tin Men don't speak English. When you say something to a Tin Man, he runs it through a filter to translate it into Tin Speak, a language he better understands. In Tin Speak, a man isn't listening to what you actually say. He's listening for what he thinks you're saying. The Tin Man assumes a woman has a hidden agenda or motive. Therefore, he listens with his guard up. For example, he's always watching for things a woman may say or do that indicate she intends to pull him into a commitment.

See Chapter 3, "How Men Translate What Women Say into Tin Speak," and Chapter 14, " 'Honey, We Need to Talk.' "

2. Why is he so afraid that I'm trying to tie him down?
Bachelorhood is the "promised land" for Tin Men. Therefore, a true Tin Man bachelor views women as possible saboteurs of his fun and carefree lifestyle. But in reality, it's not actually the woman he sees as the potential saboteur; rather, it's what he assumes she wants from him that he fears. He believes she wants to dive into a serious relationship or marriage that will deprive him of his joys in life. He regards commitment or marriage as the end of seeing his buddies. He gets cold chills as he envisions himself behind the wheel of a minivan full of screaming Little Leaguers. But make no mistake about it: Tin Men bachelors love women. But they want to have women in a way that allows them to get whatever they want from them without having any sort of commitment.

See Chapter 5, "Men vs. Women."

3. Are some women doing things that encourage men to be Tin Men?

Yes. There are lots of women who complain about men avoiding intimacy and commitments, while they are actually making it easy for men to do this. Any Tin Man player knows that if one woman won't put up with his emotional distancing in a relationship, another woman will. To be fair, there are also Tin Women. Tin Women make relationships like a prison in which a man can't have a life of his own outside the relationship. These women reinforce a Tin Man's worst fears about relationships in terms of loss of freedom and autonomy. There are also Tin Women who are just plain dangerous—they cheat, lie, and use men just as any male player would.

See Chapter 10, "The Tin Woman."

4. Is avoiding intimacy something that will go away with age?

Unfortunately, no. That's a popular misperception about Tin Men. Wisdom doesn't automatically come with age. Wisdom only comes with age when a man applies the lessons of life as he learns them. Not everyone does that. Some men have the same things happen over and over in their lives and never seem to get the point. Avoiding the vulnerability that comes with intimacy is such an ingrained part of American macho manhood that some men find it difficult to let go of that mind-set. But there is hope because ultimately all human beings need love and intimacy. And that's what keeps the Tin Man, even for the most DIE-Hard Tin Man, on his quest.

See Chapter 5, "Men vs. Women."

5. Why is it so easy for Tin Men to be sexual but not intimately connected?

A Tin Man doesn't perceive sex as an intimate connection. Rather, he sees sex as one of the biggest outlets for his ego. For that reason, Tin Men desensitize themselves from the intimacy of sex and instead look at it much the same way one would look at a sport. They see women as challenges. They see sex as a score. Tin Men are egotistical and selfish about sex. Even if they are great lovers, their motive is satisfaction of themselves or to bolster their ego. For Tin Men (or Tin Women), sex isn't even connected to intimacy. They regard the two as totally different things. Only after they begin to recover from that lifestyle do they begin to see how they've been fooling themselves and the damage they've done to themselves and others.

See Chapter 8, "Sex: The Sweet Illusion."

6. What will happen if I give a Tin Man an ultimatum about getting serious in a relationship?

Ultimatums are a bad idea. You don't ever really win with an ultimatum. One of two things happen after you give a Tin Man an ultimatum. He may give in to your demands out of fear of losing you; for example, marry you. Or, at the other extreme, he may leave you. If he gives in to your demands, it may likely be one of those cases in which you should be careful what you ask for. That's because he's agreed to your demands just to appease you. He may start to see the relationship as a deal he's made with you. And in reality he may be no more committed now than he was before the ultimatum. This can really backfire because he may feel that as long as he satisfies his end of the "deal," he doesn't have to be intimately involved in the relationship. Instead, he'll see himself as just filling the role of boyfriend or husband. But he won't really be in that role in spirit, and that can bring about an entirely new set of problems.

See Chapter 5, "Men vs. Women."

7. If I shower a Tin Man with love and affection, will that change him?

The Tin Man's issues aren't yours to solve. If a man changes because of something someone else has done, he isn't a completely changed man. Beware of changes that seem to come only because of you—they are probably temporary, or at best built on a shaky foundation. Most of the time when a man changes for a woman, he won't be able to sustain the change. Or, if he does, he may resent her for it. True change comes only from inner motivation to improve ourselves. In terms of helping a man change, the only thing a woman can do is have a positive influence on a man's behavior while remembering that any actual change is up to him.

See Chapter 13, "A Woman's Touch."

8. I've been dating a Tin Man for two years now. He considers us a serious couple, but he doesn't want to get married. Why?

He probably has you in the "girlfriend for life" category. Women in this category represent the old saying "Why buy the cow when you can get the milk for free?" If he's a DIE-Hard Tin Man and receiving all the comforts and privileges of a relationship, yet not having to be fully committed, he sees no reason to take on the responsibilities that come with marriage. But also consider this: Is it time to reevaluate your relationship? Maybe you and he want different things. He may want a steady relationship that doesn't lead to the altar, and you may be dreaming of marriage. Are you two on the same page?

See Chapter 5, "Men vs. Women."

9. Do Tin Men even have emotional needs?

Yes, men have strong emotional needs. By observing the behavior of Tin Men, some women may find that difficult to believe, but it's true. It's natural and human to have emotions. And all of us want our emotional needs met. Though Tin Men have spent their lives learning to suppress these needs, they remain within him nonetheless. When those emotional needs aren't met, they surface in other ways: Promiscuity, addictions, and violence, for example, are often rooted in unaddressed emotional issues. The issue for Tin Men, therefore, is to learn to connect with their own emotional needs. This means, among other things, accepting the vulnerability that comes with intimate connections. Only then can they begin to have meaningful and wholly satisfying relationships with women.

See Chapter 1, "What's a Tin Man?"

10. Why did he suddenly disappear when he said he was interested in having a relationship?

Many a Tin Men will tell a woman at the onset of meeting her that he is looking for a relationship. Why? Some are saying it because they think it is what a woman wants to hear. Some are trying to gain a woman's trust to get her into bed. And some actually mean it. But many of these Tin Men seem to disappear into thin air after a while, and here are three of the typical reasons:

1. He has got what he wanted from the woman (for example, sex).
2. He feels that getting what he wants will require too great an investment of his time and energy.
3. He was starting to feel that he wanted to be more intimately connected, and that feeling was too emotionally hot to handle.

See Chapter 2, "How to Recognize Tin Speak."

REALITY CHECKS

Quick Reference

Reality Check #1: Men and women aren't intended to be exactly the same. We're complementary opposites. (Chapter One, page 12)

Reality Check #2: There comes a time when there are no victims, only volunteers. (Chapter Two, page 21)

Reality Check #3: It's not always about what someone else does wrong to us, as much as it's about what we are going to do right for ourselves. (Chapter Two, page 22)

Reality Check #4: A good relationship has everything to do with timing. (Chapter Two, page 26)

Reality Check #5: Personal relationships aren't intended to be battlefields. (Chapter Six, page 62)

Reality Check #6: Love starts from the inside and works outward, while lust only exists on the outside. (Chapter Eight, page 87)

Reality Check #7: Cheating is often a symptom of a larger problem in the cheater's life and/or relationship. (Chapter Eight, page 88)

Reality Check #8: You will not die without sex. But you will perish without love. (Chapter Eight, page 90)

Reality Check #9: Some people find that blaming others for their problems is a safe and convenient way to avoid self-improvement. (Chapter Nine, page 95)

Reality Check #10: A person must want to change before anyone can help him or her. (Chapter Twelve, page 127)

Reality Check #11: Release equals peace. (Chapter Twelve, page 129)

Reality Check #12: Tolerating unacceptable behavior isn't love. (Chapter Thirteen, page 137)

Reality Check #13: When two half people get together, they make one whole mess. (Chapter Thirteen, page 137)

Reality Check #14: Don't play the role of parent in your relationship. (Chapter Thirteen, page 140)

Reality Check #15: A single and complete person is happier than a person who is spiritually and emotionally suffocating in a toxic relationship. (Chapter Thirteen, page 145)

Reality Check #16: Communication is about sharing feelings and emotions, not fighting. (Chapter Fourteen, page 147)

Reality Check #17: An apology is a powerful remedy. (Chapter Fourteen, page 153)

Reality Check #18: Forgiveness gives you peace of mind. (Chapter Fourteen, page 154)

Books, Movies, and Plays

with Tin Man— and Tin Woman—
Related Issues

Each of the following explores many of the issues presented in this book. I think you'll find all of the information beneficial to the personal growth of both men and women. Books are listed alphabetically by author name. Movies and plays are alphabetical by title.

BOOKS THAT INCLUDE TIN MAN— AND TIN WOMAN—RELATED TOPICS

Live Your Dreams, Les Brown (Avon)

Why Women Live Longer Than Men, Royda Crose, Ph.D. (Jossey-Bass)

Secrets About Men Every Woman Should Know, Barbara De Angelis, Ph.D. (Doubleday)

Why Men Are the Way They Are, Warren Farrell, Ph.D. (Berkley Publishing)

Men's Health for Dummies, Charles Inlander & The People's Medical Society (IDG Books)

The Lady, Her Lover and Her Lord, Bishop T. D. Jakes (Putnam)

Brothers on the Mend, Ernest Johnson (Simon & Schuster)

Brothers, Lust and Love, William July (Doubleday)

Fire in the Belly, Sam Keene, Ph.D. (Bantam)

What Makes the Great Great, Dennis Kimbro, Ph.D. (Doubleday)

I Don't Want to Talk About It, Terrence Real, Ph.D. (Fireside)

Ten Stupid Things Men Do to Mess Up Their Lives, Dr. Laura Schlessinger (Harper Perennial)

Ten Stupid Things Women Do to Mess Up Their Lives, Dr. Laura Schlessinger (Harper Perennial)

A Path to Healing, Dr. Andrea Sullivan, N.D. (Doubleday)

Come Before Winter and . . . Share My Hope, Charles "Chuck" Swindoll (Living Books)

Sisterfriends, Jewel Diamond Taylor (Quiet Time Publishing)

In the Meantime, Iyanla Vanzant (Simon & Schuster)

Spirit of a Man, Iyanla Vanzant (HarperCollins)

Spontaneous Healing, Andrew Weil, M.D. (Fawcett)

TIN MAN MOVIES

All titles are available on video.

Beautiful Girls

Boomerang

The Brothers McMullen

Distinguished Gentleman

Mo' Better Blues

Mr. Mom

Multiplicity

Nutty Professor (1996 version)

The Preacher's Wife

Rain Man

Swingers

Trading Places

The Truth About Cats and Dogs

Wall Street

When Harry Met Sally

The Wizard of Oz

TIN WOMAN MOVIES

Disclosure

How Stella Got Her Groove Back

The Joy Luck Club

Mother

Passion Fish

Waiting to Exhale

PLAYS WITH TIN MAN–RELATED THEMES

Death of a Salesman, Arthur Miller

Also available on video in a film adaptation directed by Voker Schlondorff; featuring Dustin Hoffman

Much Ado About Nothing, William Shakespeare

Also available on video in a film adaptation directed by Kenneth Branagh; featuring Kenneth Branagh, Michael Keaton, Keanu Reeves, Emma Thompson, and Denzel Washington

Othello, William Shakespeare

Also available on video in its most recent film adaptation directed by Oliver Parker; featuring Laurence Fishburne

Planning a Discussion

Each of the following discussion topics offers a number of interesting and engaging angles. To make your discussions more interesting and diverse, try one of these approaches:

- Select a moderator. Have the moderator read the topic and the relevant parts of the selected chapter(s) aloud. Then have the moderator field questions. When using this format, limit each person to one question. Also, limit discussion to no more than a few minutes per issue.

- Host a panel discussion. Invite experts, authors, and celebrities to sit on your panel. Select a moderator and have them pose several questions to the panel. Then open it to the audience. But there's also another way you can do the panel. You don't have to invite people outside your organization. The panel can be just as entertaining and enlightening when the panelists are people from within your organization who have interesting and diverse opinions.

- Have a casual discussion among friends. Select topics to discuss and exchange ideas and opinions.

DISCUSSION TOPICS

Here are twenty-five hot discussion topics for book clubs, discussion groups, social gatherings, and parties.

To help give background and ideas for discussions, specific chapters are referenced for each issue. But these discussions work best when customized to your group, not as straight from the book readings. Use what's here as ideas for your own creative and enlightening discussions.

Issue #1 *Mamby-Pamby or Sensitive and Manly?*
Discussion points: Should there be boundaries for male expressions of emotions? Are there such things as appropriate ways for men to show their emotions? Can women handle men showing their emotions?
See the chapter "What's a Tin Man?"

Issue #2 *Tin Speak: Do Men Say What They Mean?*
Discussion points: Why do some men have difficulty expressing themselves through words? Do most men have difficulty expressing their emotions through words?
See the chapter "How to Recognize Tin Speak."

Issue #3 *What Women Say, What Men Hear*
Discussion points: Do women say one thing but mean another, then blame men for not understanding? Do women expect men to be mind readers? The issue of the word "no" when it comes to sex. Why do men often feel blamed when women want to discuss problems?
See the chapter "How Men Translate What Women Say into 'Tin Speak.' "

Issue #4 " *'Honey, We Need to Talk'* "
Discussion points: How can couples discuss hot issues such as finance, sex, and other problems without becoming defensive or argumentative?
See the chapter " 'Honey, We Need to Talk.' "

Issue #5 *Bachelorhood: A Dream Come True?*
Discussion points: Is bachelorhood about dating as many women as possible? Should a bachelor live wildly and "try to get it all out of his system"? What makes a man want to settle down? How can bachelors define their own lives in the face of stereotypes about single men?

See the chapters "Men vs. Women," "Sex: The Sweet Illusion," and "Special Message #5: To the Young Guys."

Issue #6 *What Causes So Many Men to Avoid Commitments in Relationships?*
Discussion points: What's behind the reservations so many men seem to have about commitments? What does it take for a man to be comfortable with commitment? Are male and female goals in relationships different?
See the chapters "Men vs. Women," "Checking for Vital Signs: Emotional Numbness in Men," "Feminine Tin Speak," and "The Tin Woman."

Issue #7 *Are Men and Women at War?*
Discussion points: Do men and women compete for power in relationships? What causes a couple to compete for power? Does one person need to be the leader of the relationship? How can couples achieve a healthy interdependence?
See the chapters "Men vs. Women" and " 'Honey, We Need to Talk.' "

Issue #8 *How Important Is Sex?*
Discussion points: What's the true importance of sex in a relationship? How has the value of sex been overstated? How can sex interfere with or prevent the establishment of real intimacy in a relationship?
See the chapter "Sex: The Sweet Illusion."

Issue #9 *Celibacy*
Discussion points: How does one date or have relationships while celibate? What's the appropriate time and way to tell someone you're dating that sex will not be a part of your relationship with them? How should you tell them?
See the chapter "Sex: The Sweet Illusion."

Issue #10 *Living with Difficult People*
Discussion points: How much should you tolerate from someone?
How do you tell your significant other that he/she is driving you
crazy?
See the chapter "Honey: We Need to Talk."

Issue #11 *Should Little Boys Cry?*
Discussion points: What does our society teach little boys about
manhood? Do we teach boys that masculinity is about power and
domination? How can boys be taught to be connected with their
feelings while retaining their developing masculinity?
See the chapter "Tin Man Jr.: How Boys Grow Up to Be Tin
Men."

Issue #12 *Training and Tolerating*
Discussion points: Do women unwittingly participate in the creation and maintenance of Tin Men through what they teach boys
and what they tolerate from men? What role does the history of
women play in the beliefs many women have about manhood?
See the chapters "Tin Man Jr.: How Boys Grow Up to Be Tin
Men," "Feminine Tin Speak," and "The Tin Woman."

Issue #13 *What Makes a Father?*
Discussion points: How can some men create children and then
walk out of their lives? Does the true definition of fatherhood
transcend biological ties? What specific issues are faced by stepfa-
thers? What specific issues are faced by adopting fathers?
See the chapter "Tin Man Jr.: How Boys Grow Up to Be Tin
Men."

Issue #14 *You Can't Change a Man*
Discussion points: What things can women do to influence positive change in men? How does a woman avoid harming herself

when involved with a man who's living a self-destructive lifestyle?
Does the desire to nurture sometimes backfire on women? When
is it time to leave the relationship?
See the chapter "A Woman's Touch."

Issue #15 *Today's Woman*
Discussion points: What effect have the social changes of the
eighties and nineties had on women in relationships, motherhood,
and careers? How is life different for women of today as opposed
to women of the fifties or sixties? What are some advantages for
today's women? What are some disadvantages for today's
women?
See the chapter "Special Message 1: To the Women Who Love
Us."

Issue #16 *Women Who Avoid Intimacy*
Discussion points: What types of women avoid intimacy? What
makes a woman avoid intimacy? How can a woman overcome a
fear of intimacy?
See the chapters "Feminine Tin Speak" and "The Tin Woman."

Issue #17 *Why Is "Doctor" a Dirty Word for So Many Men?*
Discussion points: Why do men go to the doctor less than women?
What are health issues faced by men that tend to be ignored?
See the chapter "Macho-cide: Warning! Being a Tin Man Can Be
Dangerous to Your Health!"

Issue #18 *The Many Faces of Addiction*
Discussion points: How do people become addicted to food, alcohol, chemical substances, sex, or smoking? How can a person
break the chains of addiction?
See the chapters "Basic Types of Tin Men" and "Sex: The Sweet Illusion."

Issue #19 *You Are What You Eat*

Discussion points: How can we eat healthy foods on our busy schedules? Fast food is convenient, but how nutritious is it? Reading the labels; what's in the foods you eat? What is the significance of organic produce and free-range meats?

See the chapter "Macho-cide: Warning! Being a Tin Man Can Be Dangerous to Your Health!"

Issue #20 *The Big Crash*

Discussion points: Is your lifestyle unhealthy for your mind, body, and soul? Do you feel yourself slowly being burned out? What are some ways you can change your life?

See the chapters "Macho-cide: Warning! Being a Tin Man Can Be Dangerous to Your Health!" and "Twenty-eight Ways to Change Your Life, Right Now!"

Issue #21 *Changing Your Friends*

Discussion points: How do you know a person is really your friend? Are your friendships sources of strength or draining your energy? Do you have jealous friends or friends who discourage your progress? How can you find new supportive and whole friends?

See the chapter "Twenty-eight Ways to Change Your Life, Right Now!"

Issue #22 *Take a Break or Have a Breakdown?*

Discussion points: How do you know when you've had enough stress? What can you do to alleviate stress in your life? What can you do to relax yourself in the face of stress?

See the chapters "Macho-cide: Warning! Being a Tin Man Can Be Dangerous to Your Health!," "How the Tin Man Can Change," and "Twenty-eight Ways to Change Your Life, Right Now!"

Issue #23 *Is Your Job Killing You?*
Discussion points: What are some warning signs that your job is killing you? Are you fulfilled by your work or drained by it? Do you need a new job or complete career change? How can you change jobs or careers while maintaining your financial obligations?
See the chapters "Checking for Vital Signs: Emotional Numbness in Men" and "Building the Bridge to Intimacy, One Step at a Time."

Issue #24 *The Love of Money*
Discussion points: How far should we go in the pursuit of money? What challenges will money solve? What things will money not solve?
See the chapter "Basic Types of Tin Men."

Issue #25 *Living a Spiritually Based Life*
Discussion points: What is a spiritually based life? Why does it often follow a crash in life? Does living spiritually mean you'll have no fun?
See the chapters "How the Tin Man Can Change" and "Building the Bridge to Intimacy, One Step at a Time."

WHERE TO GO FOR HELP

National Clearing House for Alcohol and Drug Information
P.O. Box 2345
Rockville, MD 20847-2345
1-800-729-6686
www.health.org

National Domestic Violence Hotline
P.O. Box 161810
Austin, TX 78716
1-800-799-SAFE
       (7233)
TTY for the hearing-impaired: 1-800-787-3224
www.ndvh.org

National Sexually Transmitted Disease Hotline
P.O. Box 13827
Research Triangle Park, NC 27709
1-800-227-8922
www.ashastd.org

National Institute of Mental Health
(information on depression, anxiety, compulsions, posttraumatic
stress disorders, etc.)
6001 Executive Blvd, Room 8184, MSC 9663
Bethesda, MD 20892-9663
1-800-421-4211
www.nimh.nih.gov

CDC National HIV/AIDS Hotline
American Social Health Association
P.O. Box 13827

Research Triangle Park, NC 27709
1-800-342-AIDS
        (2437)
www.cdcnpin.org

National Mentoring Partnership
1400 I Street NW
Washington, DC 20005
1-877-Be A Ment
    (232-6368)
www.mentoring.org

Prostate Health Council/American Foundation for
Urologic Disease
1128 N Charles St
Baltimore, MD 21201
1-800-242-2383
www.prostatehealth.com

National Council on Sexual Addiction and Compulsivity
1090 Northchase Parkway, Suite 200 South
South Marietta, GA 30067
1-770-989-9754
www.ncsac.org

Web Sites for Men's Issues

On-Line Magazines
Men's Voices Journal
www.vix.com/menmag

A Man's Life
www.manslife.com

Men's Health Information
Men's Health Network
www.menshealthnetwork.org

Yahoo
www.dir.yahoo.com/health

The Black Health Net
www.blackhealthnet.com

Fatherhood
National Fatherhood Initiative
www.fatherhood.org

Fathering magazine
www.fathermag.com

WILLIAM JULY:
ONLINE AND IN PERSON

Understanding the Tin Man *Online*

www.williamjuly.com

• Send e-mail directly to William July.
• Keep posted on tour information and events.
• Read William July's online column, "Positive Energy."
• Participate in discussions about the issues in
  Understanding the Tin Man.
• Participate in opinion polls.
• Read an excerpt from William July's previous bestseller,
  *Brothers, Lust and Love: Thoughts on Manhood, Sex, and
  Romance*.

Book William July to Speak at Your College, Church, or Special Event

For booking information contact:

The Positive Energy Company
P.O. Box 62027
Houston, TX 77205-2027
NACA, Associate Member

713-801-3450

www.williamjuly.com

PERMISSIONS

Royda Crose, Ph.D., *Why Women Live Longer Than Men*. Copyright © 1997 by Jossey-Bass Inc., Publishers. Reprinted by permission of Jossey-Bass Publishers.

Jewel Diamond Taylor, *Sisterfriends*. Copyright © 1998 by Jewel Diamond Taylor. Reprinted by permission of Quiet Time Publishing.

Iyanla Vanzant, *In The Meantime*. Copyright © 1998 by Iyanla Vanzant. Reprinted by permission of Simon & Schuster.

Marianne Williamson, *A Return to Love*. Copyright © 1992 by Marianne Williamson. Reprinted by permission of HarperCollins Publishers, Inc.

Dr. Laura C. Schlessinger, *Ten Stupid Things Men Do to Mess Up Their Lives*. Copyright © 1997 by Dr. Laura C. Schlessinger. Reprinted by permission of HarperCollins Publishers, Inc.

Sam Keen, Ph.D., *Fire in the Belly*. Copyright © 1991 by Sam Keen. Reprinted by permission of Bantam Books.

Patrick Carnes, Ph.D., *Out of the Shadows*. Copyright © 1992 by Patrick Carnes, Ph.D. Reprinted by permission of the Carnes Hazelden Foundation.

Dr. Andrea D. Sullivan, N.D., *A Path to Healing*. Copyright © 1998 by Andrea D. Sullivan. Reprinted by permission of Doubleday.

John Gray, Ph.D., *Men Are from Mars, Women Are from Venus*. Copyright © 1992 by John Gray. Reprinted by permission of Harper-Collins Publishers, Inc.